D1403570

3852 6576

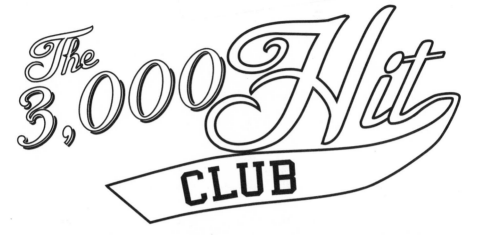

The 3,000 Hit CLUB

STORIES OF BASEBALL'S GREATEST HITTERS

FRED McMANE

WITH

STUART SHEA

East Baton Rouge Parish Library
Baton Rouge, Louisiana

SPORTS
PUBLISHING

Copyright © 2000, 2012 by Fred McMane

New material © 2012 by Skyhorse Publishing, Inc.

All Rights Reserved. No part of this book may be reproduced in any manner without the express written consent of the publisher, except in the case of brief excerpts in critical reviews or articles. All inquiries should be addressed to Sports Publishing, 307 West 36th Street, 11th Floor, New York, NY 10018.

Sports Publishing books may be purchased in bulk at special discounts for sales promotion, corporate gifts, fund-raising, or educational purposes. Special editions can also be created to specifications. For details, contact the Special Sales Department, Sports Publishing, 307 West 36th Street, 11th Floor, New York, NY 10018 or sportspubbooks@skyhorsepublishing.com.

Sports Publishing® is a registered trademark of Skyhorse Publishing, Inc.®, a Delaware corporation.

Visit our website at www.sportspubbooks.com

10 9 8 7 6 5 4 3 2 1

Library of Congress Cataloging-in-Publication Data is available on file.

ISBN: 978-1-61321-060-4

Printed in the United States of America

Table of Contents

The 3,000 Hit CLUB

Pete Rose

Ranking: 1st
Hit Total: 4,256

Courtesy of Cincinnati Reds

L ee Weyer had been the third-base umpire the night that Henry Aaron hit his 715th home run to break Babe Ruth's record in 1973. Now here he was, 12 years later, crouched behind home plate, about to witness another historic baseball achievement that had once seemed unattainable.

Three years earlier, Weyer had made a promise to Pete Rose that he would be behind the plate for the game in which Rose broke Ty Cobb's record for most career hits. At the time, the record appeared out of Rose's reach. Rose was 41 then and nearing the end of his brilliant career.

But the fire in the belly that had driven Rose to stardom still burned brightly, and Weyer knew Rose would not quit until he had broken the record. Now the night had arrived. Rose, 44, was dead even with Cobb at 4,191 hits. No longer an everyday player, he had returned to the Reds in 1984 as a player/manager and had pecked away at Cobb's mark until this moment.

The crowd of 47,237 was on its feet when Rose stepped to the plate with one out and nobody on in the first inning against San Diego's Eric Show. Rose took a pitch for ball one, then fouled the next pitch back. Show's next pitch was slightly inside, raising the count to 2-1—a hitter's count. Show delivered a slider that began to break toward the inside corner. But before it got there, Rose's black bat whipped across the plate and met the ball solidly. The ball soared on a line toward left-center field and fell to the Astroturf about 15 feet in front of Padres left fielder Carmelo Martinez.

As the ball hit the ground, fireworks began shooting off, and a big "4,192!" flashed on the scoreboard. Reds players began pouring out of the dugout, along with Rose's 15-year-old son, Petey, and surrounded baseball's new all-time hit king.

Peter Edward Rose was a modern-day Ty Cobb. He played the game with a great intensity, and his work ethic and drive to win were exemplary.

"I don't give just 100 percent because some guy opposite me might be giving that much," Rose once said. "If you have a guy equal in ability to me, I'm gonna beat him, because I'll try harder. That guy ain't got no chance."

Not only was Rose baseball's all-time hit leader, but he was a catalyst on three world-championship teams and set 34 major league or National League records. He was an NL Most Valuable Player, a World Series MVP, a three-time NL batting champion and one of the most entertaining players of his era.

Yet he also brought discredit to the game. In 1989, he was banished from baseball by then-commissioner A. Bartlett Giamatti for conduct detrimental to baseball. The charge was betting on baseball games, including those of his team, the Cincinnati Reds.

By being placed on the ineligible list, he cannot be elected to the Hall of Fame. He thus remains the only member of baseball's 3,000 hit club eligible for election who is not in the Cooperstown, N.Y., shrine.

There was never really any actual proof made public that Rose bet on baseball games, and he categorically denied it. Yet, he admitted to a gambling addiction, and in an agreement made with baseball, Rose accepted his banishment from the sport. However, he set as his remaining lifetime goal to get off the list and into the Hall of Fame.

As a baseball player, Rose is the perfect example of the individual who made the very most of what he had. Although limited in natural skills, he worked hard to become one of the sport's all-time great players.

Rose played 24 seasons in the major leagues, 19 of them with the Cincinnati Reds (1963-1978, 1984-1986). He also spent four seasons with the Philadelphia Phillies (1979-83) and part of a season with the Montreal Expos (1984).

He got his first major league hit on April 13, 1963, and more than 22 years later, on September 11, 1985, he broke a record nobody thought possible—Cobb's career record for most hits. Rose finished his career with 4,256 career hits and 10 other major league records. Remarkably, he notched more than 1,000 hits after the age of 38.

In addition to most hits, he owns the career records for games played (3,562), most at-bats (14,053), most singles (3,315), most total bases by a switch-hitter (5,752), most seasons of 200 or more hits (10), most consecutive seasons of 100 or more hits (23), most seasons of 600 or more at-bats (17), most seasons of 150 or more games (17), most seasons of 100 or more games (23) and most winning games (1,972).

He also is the only player in major league history to play more than 500 games at five different positions. Rose played first base, second base, third base, left field and right field during his career.

Born on April 14, 1941, in Cincinnati, Rose was the third of four children of Harry, known as "Pete," and La Verne Rose. As a youngster, Pete favored football—which was his father's sport—over baseball, but he was not selected to try out for the varsity as a sophomore, because he was considered too small.

This rejection hurt Pete badly, and he lost interest in school. As a result, he flunked out, and it took him five years to graduate. He did play football for two years in high school, but he was not eligible to play his senior year because he was too old. Even though he weighed only 150 pounds at graduation, he was tough and a fiery competitor and was offered a football scholarship to play at Ohio's Miami University. But by then, he had his heart set on playing professional baseball.

However, only two teams, the Baltimore Orioles and the Cincinnati Reds, expressed interest in him. The Reds were impressed with Rose's dedication and ambition but were concerned about his lack of size. However, Buddy Bloebaum, Rose's uncle and a Reds scout, told the front office that the men in Rose's family matured late and convinced Reds officials to take a chance with him.

The Reds signed Rose to a modest bonus and assigned him to Geneva (N.Y.) of the New York-Pennsylvania League. Unlike many switch-hitters, Rose had been batting from both sides of the plate from an early age. Still, he found the adjustment to pro ball very difficult.

He struggled in his first year, batting only .277 while also experiencing great difficulty at second base. But, just as Bloebaum had predicted, Rose began to mature physically. He worked for the Railway Express Agency, lifting crates during the off-season, and over the next several years he gradually matured into a muscular 5-11, 190-pounder.

During his next two minor league seasons, Rose hit well over .300, and in 1963 the Reds made him their regular second baseman. Rose brought to the Reds a desire that few in baseball had seen in many years. With a crewcut and gung-ho attitude, he resembled a Marine in boot camp.

It was during an exhibition game against the New York Yankees that Rose got the nickname that would signify his career, "Charlie Hustle." Whitey Ford, the great Yankees pitcher, hung the moniker on Rose after watching him run full speed to first base following a walk. Rose had been taught to do that by his father, who had seen Cardinals outfielder Enos Slaughter do it and admired it.

"Look at that 'Charlie Hustle,'" Ford had said to teammate Mickey Mantle after watching Rose sprint to first base. It was a term that big leaguers used to brand someone as a showoff. But Rose wasn't showing off. It was his style of play, and it would become his trademark.

Rose was not easily accepted by his Reds teammates in his first few years with the team. For one thing, he had replaced Don Blasingame, a popular player, at second base. Also, his brashness and self-confidence did not sit well with some of the veterans on the team. Rose's best friends on the team became black stars Frank Robinson and Vada Pinson.

Rose batted .273 in his first season with the Reds and was named the National League's Rookie of the Year. But he still had many deficiencies at second base, especially going to his right and making the double play.

He started slowly at the plate in 1964 and was benched in August. After returning to the starting lineup, he hit well and raised his season's average to .269, but he knew he was going to have to work harder at improving his game.

That winter he went to play in the Venezuelan League. He put in many hours in improving his fielding skills and working on his batting stroke. By the time the major league season began, Rose was a vastly im- proved player. He batted over .300 for the first of 15 seasons in 1965 and collected a league-leading 209 hits, including 35 doubles, 11 triples and 11 homers. His fielding improved, too, although he was never more than an adequate second baseman in the four years he played the position.

It was his take-charge attitude and desire to win that set him apart from most other players. His aggressiveness, head-first slides on the bases, ability to come through with a big hit in the clutch and a never-say-die attitude made him a fan favorite and began to earn him the respect of his teammates.

Before long, Rose was the unequivocal leader of the Reds. In 1967, he demonstrated his versatility and team spirit by shifting to the outfield. "If I can make the All-Star team as an infielder, I can make it as an out- fielder," he said. And he did.

As an outfielder in 1968 and 1969, he won consecutive NL batting titles with .335 and .348 averages. In 1973, he won another batting title with a .338 average and also was named the NL's MVP. In 1975, he was the World Series MVP while leading the Reds to the first of two succes- sive world championships. After signing with the Phillies as a free agent following the 1978 season, he helped lead them to a World Series title in 1980—the club's first in history.

In 1978, Rose tied the NL record by hitting in 44 consecutive games. On May 5 of that year, he became the youngest player to reach the 3,000-hit plateau with a single off Montreal's Steve Rogers. Three years later he would set the NL record for most hits as a member of the Phillies.

After the 1983 season, in which he helped get the Phillies into another World Series, he signed with the Expos as a free agent. He got his 4,000th hit on April 13 against the Phillies, but he was used only sparingly by Montreal after an early-season slump. In August, the Expos sent him back to Cincinnati, where he became player/manager of the Reds. It was in Cincinnati on September 11, 1985, that Rose singled off San Diego's Eric Show to break Cobb's career hit record.

He proved to be a fine manager, too, guiding the Reds to an 89-72 record in 1985. But it was also as the Reds' manager that his troubles with gambling finally surfaced.

There is no absolute proof that Rose bet on baseball games. There is, however, considerable circumstantial evidence that Rose placed bets on baseball games, including games involving the Reds.

Almost all of this indirect evidence is derived from former friends and associates of Rose. This was a group of men he first met in 1984 at a local gym in Cincinnati. They were mostly men on the outside fringe of the sports world. Some were bodybuilders who had built themselves up on steroids and were affiliated with bookmakers.

These men included Tommy Gioiosa, Donald Stenger, Mike Fry and later Paul Janszen. Through these associates, Rose met and dealt with Ron Peters and Steve Chavashore, a pair of bookmakers who took Rose's bets.

Gioiosa, Janszen and Peters have all claimed that Rose bet on baseball. All three were convicted felons and each was involved in illegal gambling, drug dealing (cocaine and steroids) and income tax evasion.

Rose met Gioiosa in Florida in 1978 and the two forged a friendship that would last more than 10 years. Gioiosa moved to Cincinnati and lived with Rose and his family, and it was Gioiosa who introduced Rose to the group of bodybuilders at the local Cincinnati gym where Gioiosa worked out.

In February 1990, after refusing to give a deposition to the baseball officials investigating Rose, and nearly six months after Rose's banishment, Gioiosa claimed on a Cincinnati television talk show that Rose had bet on baseball games. By then, however, Gioiosa and Rose were no longer friends.

It was possible that Gioiosa was telling the truth. But it was also possible that he was being vindictive, paying Rose back for having taken advantage of him. Gioiosa claimed that Rose frequently borrowed money from him but never paid it back.

Janszen also implicated Rose in later questioning by investigators. But he too had been owed money by Rose and may have been trying to get even by lying to the investigators.

In March 1988, Janszen was being investigated in connection with an FBI probe into drug dealing and income tax evasion. Janszen began cooperating with the investigators, and he also needed to get back some of the more than $40,000 he had lent Rose over the past year. But Rose, according to Janszen, would only pay back $10,000. The rest of the money, which Janszen felt Rose owed him, would not be forthcoming.

Janszen felt betrayed by Rose and began answering questions about Rose's gambling activities to FBI investigators. Janszen pleaded guilty to a charge of income tax evasion, and because of his cooperation he received a light sentence of six months in a halfway house. During this period, he also talked to John Dowd, who was leading major league baseball's investigation into Rose's gambling habits. Janszen told Dowd that Rose had bet on baseball games. But he went one step further than Gioiosa. Janszen also provided documentary evidence in the form of betting sheets that were written by Rose.

Another Rose associate, Ron Peters, also provided testimony to Dowd. Peters was a Franklin, Ohio, bookmaker who had taken Rose's bets first through Gioiosa and then from Janszen. Peters claimed that in 1987, Rose would sometimes bet up to $30,000 a day on various major league baseball games. Peters was convicted of drug dealing and tax evasion, in part because of the testimony of Janszen. As an FBI informant, Janszen secretly taped conversations he had had with Peters.

Janszen's and Peters' testimony, deemed accurate by Dowd, formed the basis of the May 1989 report to commissioner Giamatti, known as the "Dowd Report." This report was released to the public in late June, and it consisted of 225 pages and an additional 2,000 pages of transcribed interviews, depositions and documents. Janszen's testimony, combined with telephone records and the betting sheets, convinced Giamatti that Rose had bet on baseball games.

Rose, naturally, thought the Dowd Report was nonsense. "It was a hatchet job, a piece of crap. I'm guilty of one thing in this whole mess, and that's that I was a poor selector of friends," he said.

Rose did admit on a national television talk show that he was a compulsive gambler. The evidence presented to Giamatti certainly looked to be incriminating, and the commissioner had no choice but to issue the ban. Betting on baseball is considered a cardinal sin, and Rose was forced to pay for his transgression.

The day after banning Rose, Giamatti held a news conference where he said:

"The matter of Mr. Rose is now closed. It will be debated and discussed. Let no one think it did not hurt baseball. The hurt will pass, however, as the great glory of the game asserts itself and a resilient institution goes forward. Let it also be clear that no individual is superior to the game."

Unfortunately for Rose, things got even worse. The Internal Revenue Service cracked down on him for income tax evasion in 1990, and he was found guilty and sentenced to eight months in jail. He was released on January 7, 1991.

Since his release from prison, Rose has tried hard to get baseball to rescind its ban against him. He is not allowed to attend any major league function or be affiliated with any major league baseball team. Instead, he supports himself with a national radio sports talk show, a restaurant in Florida and income from baseball card shows and other endorsements.

"I just can't imagine I'm not going to get reinstated," he said. "I gotta make the Hall of Fame. It's not right for the game of baseball."

Ty Cobb

Ranking: 2nd
Hit Total: 4,189

AP/Wide World Photos

Lou Criger had seen this type before. As the starting catcher on two American League championship teams with Boston, he knew all about the brash kids who needed to be put in their place. And this young fellow, Ty Cobb, was no different.

So when a reporter sidled up to Criger before a game against the Detroit Tigers and asked him what he thought of Cobb, the Boston catcher had some rather choice words.

"This Cobb is one of those ginks with a lot of flash, but he doesn't fool me," said Criger. "Watch him wilt when the going gets tough. I'll cut him down to size."

At breakfast the next morning, Cobb saw the quote in the newspaper and became enraged.

That afternoon Cobb singled in his first at-bat and yelled at Criger, who was behind the plate, "Watch out, you big baboon! I'm going down on the first pitch."

Cobb took off on the first pitch and promptly stole second. He hollered in at Criger again, "I'm taking third on the next pitch."

On the next delivery, Cobb headed for third and slid in well ahead of Criger's throw.

"Out of my way, ice wagon. I'm coming home," Cobb screamed at Criger. As the pitcher went into his windup Cobb headed full-steam for home and beat the hurried toss to the plate.

Once again, Cobb had proven his point: Don't ever insult me or you'll pay the price.

He was irascible, mean-spirited and an avowed racist. Yet, Tyrus Raymond Cobb may have been the greatest baseball player who ever lived.

They called him "The Georgia Peach," but there was nothing peachy about his disposition. Socially, there is very little positive one can say about Ty Cobb. He was a misfit, an outcast so disliked by everyone who came in contact with him that he died practically friendless.

Psychologists may claim that Cobb's behavior is a direct result of a horrid moment in his early 20s when his mother, mistaking his father for a prowler, shot him to death. Or it could have been his father's words to him when he left home to seek a career in baseball: "Don't come back a failure."

Whatever the reason, Cobb was a very driven and angry man for most of his life. Yet, as a baseball player, he was a marvel. During his 24-year major league career, most of which was spent with the Detroit Tigers, he posted a .366 batting average, the highest of all time, and won a record 12 American League batting titles, including an incredible nine in a row from 1907 to 1915.

Standing deep in the box against left-handed pitchers and moving up on the plate against righties, he hit .316 or better in all of his big-league seasons except the first. He scored more runs than any player (2,245) and is one of only 11 players in baseball history to lead the league in batting average, home runs and runs batted in during the same season. He was the first to win the Triple Crown, accomplishing the feat in 1911 with a .377 batting average, nine home runs and 115 RBI.

He also was the first millionaire ballplayer, although it was not his talent on the ball field that made him rich, but rather his shrewdness in the stock market. He invested heavily in a soft drink named *Coca-Cola* and amassed a fortune. When he died in 1961 at the age of 74, his estate was worth $11 million.

Cobb broke into the big leagues at age 18 with a double in his first major league at-bat and finished his career at age 41 with the last of his 4,191 hits. It was a record for most career hits that lasted for more than half a century.

But there was far more to Cobb's game than mere statistics. He treated every game as if it were a war, running the bases with reckless abandon, and was willing—and some might say eager—to cause mayhem, if necessary, in order to get the upper hand on an opponent.

Violence and fighting were the only ways Cobb knew to defend his honor. He was unable to take a joke or laugh at himself, and anyone who made fun of him risked a beating. Unfortunately, blacks were more prone to such a response than whites.

A native of Narrows, Georgia, where racism was commonplace, Cobb felt blacks were inferior to the white man and could never expect equal treatment from him. There are many incidents of Cobb's mistreatment of black people. At least twice he was arrested for assault and battery on a black man and was forced to pay money to settle civil suits filed by those he attacked.

How ornery was Cobb? While Pete Rose was chasing Cobb's all-time hit record, one reporter asked Rose's opinion on what Cobb might be thinking if he was looking down on the chase.

"From what I know about him," Rose answered, pointing skyward, "he's probably not up there."

Cobb was a master psychologist. He studied opposing players, looking for a weakness. When he found it, he exploited it zealously. He would swing three bats in the on-deck circle just to show the other team his strength. He was able to hit the way he did by working himself into a hateful frenzy before each at-bat. If he could hate the pitcher, then he would go up to bat ready to humiliate the pitcher in front of all the fans in the stands.

Humiliation of the opposition was Cobb's credo. Since he viewed baseball as a war, he sought not only to beat the enemy, but also to utterly humiliate everyone he faced. It was never enough simply to win; he had to win big. He felt if he could run up the score on his opponents, they would be demoralized the next time they played and expect to be beaten again.

"Baseball is a red-blooded sport for red-blooded men. It's no pink tea, and mollycoddles had better stay out. It's a struggle for supremacy, survival of the fittest," Cobb said.

He used all kinds of tricks to annoy the opposition. To confuse pitchers, Cobb would sometimes act as if he didn't care about or even notice the pitcher. He would bend over to pick up a handful of dirt when the pitcher was beginning his delivery. This would so unravel the pitcher that he would lose his concentration and not be able to throw a strike. One time, with Eddie Cicotte on the mound, Cobb kept his back turned and talked to Sam Crawford, waiting in the on-deck circle. Cicotte walked Cobb on four pitches.

Very few batters of the era could hit fastballing Walter Johnson of the Washington Senators. Yet Cobb batted .335 lifetime against the all-time shutout leader by employing what the Tigers' outfielder said was a knowledge of *phrenology,* a system of character analysis based upon the belief that certain faculties and character traits are indicated by the configurations of the skull.

Cobb claimed that his knowledge of phrenology told him that Johnson was kind-hearted and even-tempered and was afraid to hit anyone with his pitches. So Cobb crowded the plate, and Johnson, not willing to brush

Cobb back, had to pitch him outside, where Cobb could hit the ball to the opposite field. Did Cobb really know anything about phrenology? Who knows? More than likely, Johnson was aware of his special talent and feared he might kill someone if he ever hit him in the head with his fastball.

Once on base, Cobb was at his most dangerous. He stole 892 bases, third on the all-time list, and many of them came as a way of showing up the opposition. Cobb believed the base paths belonged to him and that he had every right to do whatever he could to keep it that way. An example of this came in a game against Cleveland in June 1907 when he tripled. Instead of stopping at third, Cobb continued home, where Harry Bemis, the catcher, was waiting with the ball. Cobb lowered his shoulder and plowed Bemis over, forcing him to drop the ball. In response, Bemis picked up the ball and beat Cobb over the head with it until the umpire pulled Bemis off Cobb and ejected the catcher.

Another time, Cobb was playing against the New York Highlanders, whose gifted first baseman, Hal Chase, had a habit of throwing the ball over to third on plays where a runner would advance to third on an infield out. This was to keep the runner from rounding third. On one occasion, however, with Cobb on second after a double, Claude Rossman, an expert bunter who followed Cobb in the batting order, laid down a sacrifice bunt. Instead of stopping at third, Cobb kept running full speed toward home, and Chase, accustomed to throwing the ball to third, was completely surprised. When he tried to stop and throw to home, he threw the ball over the third baseman's head, allowing Cobb to score easily.

Cobb's favorite baserunning maneuver was going from first to third on sacrifice bunts. He perfected this skill with Rossman as the batter. While on first, Cobb would flash his own bunt sign to Rossman, then take off for second on the pitch. Rossman would bunt the ball down the third-base line, where the third baseman had to field the ball and throw to first. The shortstop was usually heading toward second to cover for the steal attempt, and so the third baseman had to field the ball and then run back to cover his own base. Often Cobb beat either the throw or the third baseman or both.

As a student of baserunning, Cobb did many things, some little, some big, that he felt gave him an advantage. He felt no edge was too small for him to exploit. He would antagonize the opposition by deliberately standing in the way of throws. He would watch the eyes of fielders to see where the ball was coming and then position himself directly in the way of the throw.

At times, Cobb used the press to help him with his psychological gamesmanship. The media often portrayed him as a "monster" who would sit in the dugout before the game, sharpening his spikes. It wasn't true, of course, but Cobb waited until after his playing days to refute the story. He felt if the opposition believed the story, they would be even more intimidated by him.

He would often get up from a slide and limp around, call time, and generally act disabled, like he wouldn't be able to give his all on the bases. With the defense's guard down, he could then run hard and catch the defense napping. He would kick each base toward the next, taking advantage of the few inches of play in the base mounts. He would sometimes jump, yell, and wave his arms at the pitcher to distract him. He perfected the hook slide, where he would hit the base with only a toe or grab it on his way by, always leaving the smallest area possible for a fielder to tag.

"Most of all, I was saddling that team with a psychological burden so that they would be muttering, 'Cobb is crazy. He'll run anytime and in any situation,'" said Cobb. "It would help give them the jitters, and they'd concentrate so much on me, they were not paying any attention to the business at hand."

Once in a game against the Athletics in Philadelphia in August 1910, he hit a high bouncing ball behind second base. He didn't even slow down as he passed first and headed toward second. He slid in safely ahead of the ball, which had been fielded and thrown too late to first and then too late to second. He then scored from second after a hard line drive ricocheted off the pitcher's glove to the second baseman, who got the out at first.

Cobb seldom made a mistake on the bases, but one of his major blunders came in the 1908 World Series against the Chicago Cubs. In Game 3, Cobb singled and announced that he would steal second on the next pitch. He did so, knocking over second baseman Joe Tinker in the process. He then stole third base. Rossman, the next batter, then walked and continued past first toward second, hoping to get the pitcher, Ed Reulbach, to make a play on him so that Cobb could score. Cobb broke for home, as he had done many times, but Reulbach threw home and Cobb was tagged out in a rundown, much to the delight of the Cubs' fans.

"My failures rarely were complete failures," Cobb said. "They were more like future investments."

Cobb's biggest embarrassment came at home on May 11, 1909, the day the Tigers hoisted the AL pennant from 1908. In the seventh inning, Cobb tried to score from second base on a bunt. However, this time, his teammate, Sam Crawford, was standing on third base and Cobb ran right past him and was called out for passing a runner. It was perhaps the worst booing he ever received at home.

The biggest controversy surrounding his baserunning came in August of 1909 in Detroit, when he tried to steal third against the Philadelphia Athletics. The throw had him beat, so he did a hook slide to his left to try to avoid the tag. Frank "Home Run" Baker, the Athletics' third baseman, reached across the base and tagged Cobb with his bare hand. Cobb's spikes on his right shoe caught Baker on his forearm and opened up a small cut. Philadelphia fans and league officials felt that Cobb had finally crossed the line. Connie Mack, the Athletics' manager, called Cobb the "dirtiest player ever." AL president Ban Johnson initially condemned him for his slide, but later said that Cobb was merely playing hard within the rules.

Philadelphia fans were outraged. Before the next Detroit visit to Philadelphia, Cobb received several death threats. When Detroit met the Athletics in Philadelphia the next time, the field was filled with almost as many police as fans, all of whom expected some kind of retaliation by the Athletics or the fans, but nothing occurred.

Cobb's aggressive baserunning style caused him repeated injuries over the years, especially abrasions from sliding on rock-hard infields. Moreover, Tigers owner Frank Navin was very cheap and often would not pay for Cobb's medical treatment when he needed it.

"I recall when Cobb played a series with each leg a mass of raw flesh," sportswriter Grantland Rice recalled. "He had a temperature of 103, and the doctors ordered him to bed for several days, but he got three hits, stole three bases, and won the game."

While baserunning seemed to come almost naturally to the speedy Georgian, Cobb had to learn to become a good hitter. He could not hit left-handers well when he first broke into organized baseball, but he worked hard at perfecting a stroke that would take left-handers to the opposite field. In 1907, two months before his 21st birthday, he won his first American League batting title.

Cobb's golden years as a hitter were in 1911 and 1912, when he hit .420 and .409. In 1911, he collected 248 hits in 146 games. He was so hot that year that he began talking about getting 300 hits and breaking the all-time average record of .492 (compiled in 1887 by Tip O'Neill in a year in which walks counted as hits). But on August 13, Cobb was diagnosed with bronchitis and had to sit out much of the rest of the season. In addition to his .420 average and 248 hits, he finished with 147 runs scored, 144 RBI, 83 stolen bases, and the league lead in doubles, triples, and slugging average. He was awarded a Chalmers car for being voted the AL MVP by the Baseball Writers Association of America.

Cobb was just as diligent about his fielding as he was about his hitting. Although not particularly a good outfielder when he first broke into the major leagues, he improved his fielding steadily throughout his career.

In 1907, he played very shallow in right field and collected 30 outfield assists, his career high. Not only did he throw out runners at second, third and home, but he also managed to throw out a few runners who failed to hustle to first base on balls hit to the outfield.

He was adept at charging ground balls to the outfield to get more power behind his throws. He also would position himself so that he was running forward when he caught fly balls in order to get off a stronger throw.

Despite Cobb's heroics on the field, the Tigers were basically underachievers during his 22 years with the club. The Tigers won only three pennants in that time, all in a row, from 1907 to 1909, but they did not win one World Series. Perhaps it was the bad chemistry Cobb created on the field and in the clubhouse. He was intensely disliked by virtually all of his teammates. It started in his rookie season when he was ostracized by his teammates because of his quiet manner, which they interpreted as conceit. Cobb had been raised to be a gentleman in the Southern tradition, but he soon found there was no place for gentility in baseball.

Cobb had fistfights with many of his teammates, but the opposition hated him even more. The Cleveland team even tried to conspire to rob Cobb of a batting title in 1910. Cobb's growing domination of the art of hitting angered many in the baseball world, because they hated to see someone like Cobb beat all the men whom people admired. One player so revered was Napoleon Lajoie, player/manager of Cleveland. Lajoie was so popular that the Cleveland team was called the "Naps" in his honor.

It had been advertised that the winner of the batting title in 1910 would receive a brand-new car, a Chalmers 30, donated by the owner of the Chalmers Motor Car Company. In early July, Lajoie had almost a .030 lead on Cobb, but by the beginning of September, Cobb had cut his deficit to .008.

Then, just before a series in Cleveland, Cobb came down with an inflamed optic nerve and missed the entire series. Many people felt he was afraid to go head-to-head with Lajoie. Once the inflammation subsided, Cobb went 5-for-6 in a doubleheader with New York and 4-for-7 over two days in Chicago. Then, with a virtually insurmountable lead, he sat out Detroit's last two games.

Lajoie needed to have a perfect last few games to beat Cobb, as the Naps finished their season in St. Louis. Jack O'Connor, the manager of St. Louis, wanted to see Lajoie win the title instead of Cobb. He therefore had his rookie third baseman Red Corriden play near the outfield grass, so that Lajoie could lay down bunts all day and beat them out. O'Connor told Corriden that he didn't want him to get hurt by a sharp line drive.

Lajoie tripled in his first at-bat, but in his next seven plate appearances, he bunted and beat out six of them for hits. He also bunted safely to shortstop for an 8-for-9 performance. He later received a telegram congratulating him on his accomplishments from several members of the Tigers.

But when league president Johnson released the official statistics, Cobb was the champion, .384944 to .384084. When the word got out about what O'Connor had done, Johnson ran him out of organized baseball. Much of the league was in uproar over what had happened. But Chalmers, enjoying the publicity, gave a car to both Cobb and Lajoie. In the years since, research has shown that Lajoie actually won, .384 to .383, but the *MacMillian Encyclopedia* still lists Cobb as the winner.

One significant thing about Cobb's career is that he brought as much fire to the game during his final season of 1928 as he did in his early years, even though his talent had clearly eroded. Playing for the Philadelphia Athletics in his last two seasons, Cobb hit .323 in 95 games in his last campaign.

His last steal of home came against Cleveland in that final season, giving him 50 for his career. Typically, he caught the Cleveland pitcher unaware, since most baseball observers considered Cobb too old for that sort of thing anymore.

When he was finally forced to retire from baseball after the 1928 season, the fall from the spotlight was a hard one. He spent the last 33 years of his life a virtual loner, drinking and smoking too much and complaining about the ineptness of the modern ballplayer.

Once at a baseball function he was asked what he thought he would hit if he played in the modern era. "Oh, about .350," Cobb replied matter-of-factly.

"Is that all?" the questioner persisted.

"Yes, but you've got to remember I'm 70 years old," Cobb answered.

Needless to say, that kind of attitude did not endear him to the new edition of baseball players either.

Cobb spent much of his retirement pursuing his off-season activities of hunting, golfing, and fishing. He also traveled extensively, both with and without his family. His other hobby was trading stocks and bonds, which increased his immense personal wealth.

Nineteen years after his career ended, so did his marriage of 39 years. He married again at 62 but that, too, ended in divorce. When his sons died young, Cobb was alone with few friends left.

One of Cobb's few thrills in retirement came in February 1936, when the first Hall of Fame election results were announced. Cobb was named on 222 of 226 ballots, far outdistancing Babe Ruth, Honus Wagner, Christy Mathewson, and Walter Johnson, the only others to earn the necessary 75 percent of votes to be elected.

Cobb's percentage of 98.2 stood as the record until pitcher Steve Carlton broke it almost 60 years later. It showed that, although many people hated Cobb, they respected the way he played and what he accomplished.

Right before he died, Cobb admitted he had made many mistakes in his life. He said he had played hard and lived hard and had no friends to show for it, and he regretted it.

His funeral was perhaps the saddest event connected with Cobb. From all of baseball, the sport that he had dominated for over 20 years, only three old players and Sid Keener from the Hall of Fame came. Many of Cobb's contemporaries had already passed away, but he had alienated most of the others, and they refused to pay him their last respects.

Hank Aaron

Ranking: 3rd
Hit Total: 3,771

AP/Wide World Photos

Most of the letters were postmarked in northern states. They were vicious and vile, full of hate and anger. They had begun arriving years earlier and now were coming in bunches in the summer of 1973 as Hank Aaron, a black man from the Deep South, closed in on a cherished baseball record, the career home run mark of the legendary Babe Ruth.

Now, as the Atlanta Braves slugger was poised to break the Babe's record of 714 home runs in April of 1974, he did so with some trepidation.

Some of the letters he was receiving were death threats:

"Dear Nigger Henry,

You are [not] going to break this record established by the great Babe Ruth if I can help it. Whites are far more superior than jungle bunnies. My gun is watching your every black move."

Hank had tied the Babe's record in his first at-bat of the season, crushing a pitch by Cincinnati's Jack Billingham over the fence for No. 714. That night he called his mother. "I'm going to save the next one for you, Mom," he said.

Now, as he left the on-deck circle on April 8, 1974, he was determined to make history despite the racist intimidations. The largest crowd in Braves history (53,775) had turned out to witness the event, and he did not want to disappoint them.

In the fourth inning, he stepped to the plate against left-hander Al Downing of the Los Angeles Dodgers. Downing's first pitch was a ball. He then tried to sneak a fastball past Aaron, which left-hander Curt Simmons once said was "like trying to sneak the sunrise past a rooster." Even at age 40, he still had powerful wrists and forearms that could whip a bat around in a millisecond. Aaron was on Downing's fastball instantly, sending it on a line 400 feet into the Braves bullpen, where it was caught by reliever Tom House. A record no one ever thought would be broken now belonged to Aaron.

As he rounded second base, two college students appeared and, for a moment, Hank thought they meant him harm. It was soon evident they were there merely to share in the moment of Aaron's historic event, but security personnel quickly grabbed them and took them away. As Aaron reached home plate, he was met by a mob—the entire Braves team surrounded him and honored baseball's new home run king.

"People say, 'I know you threw that pitch deliberately,'" Downing said years later. "But that's not true. I was there to shut them down. I was confronted with a great hitter and I challenged him. I wasn't going to let up."

Aaron would go on to hit 40 more home runs until retiring after the 1976 season with 755. Aaron still has the record—and the hate mail.

"I read the letters," he said, "because they remind me not to be surprised or hurt. They remind me what people are really like."

They called Henry Louis Aaron "Hammerin' Hank," and the name fit perfectly. In addition to the home run record, Aaron also hammered his way into the record book for knocking in the most runs (2,297) and compiling the most total bases (6,856) and extra-base hits (1,477). He ranks second in at-bats (12,364), is tied for second with Ruth in runs (2,174), and is third in hits (3,771) and games played (3,298). He is the only player to hit at least 30 homers in 15 seasons and at least 20 homers in 20 seasons. He hit at least 40 homers eight times, with a career best of 47.

Aaron also was the first player to reach 3,000 hits and 500 homers. He led the National League in homers and RBI four times each and played in 24 All-Star Games.

Though Aaron's chase of Ruth's home run record was one of the most chronicled and significant events in baseball history, he was far more than a mere slugger. He was a complete player, one who could beat you with his bat, glove, or baserunning. He won three Gold Gloves for fielding excellence and stole 240 bases.

A lifetime .305 hitter, Aaron did most of his damage for the Braves, first in Milwaukee (1954-65), then in Atlanta (1966-74), before finishing his 23-year career with the Milwaukee Brewers (1975-76).

While Aaron had great numbers, he never had much fan appeal. He was not as flashy as Willie Mays or as outspoken as Ted Williams. Aaron was considered hardworking, humble, and shy, just as Joe DiMaggio was. But while those qualities made DiMaggio a hero playing in New York, they made Aaron an enigma. Aaron was often overlooked as one of the game's greats until he took off on his chase of Ruth's record. Playing in the small-market areas of Milwaukee and Atlanta no doubt hurt his national popularity.

"Willie was more exciting," said Don Newcombe, a pitcher for the Brooklyn Dodgers. "Hank was laid-back, but he could do everything Willie could. As a pitcher, I had more respect for Hank. Willie was a first-ball hitter. You didn't know what Hank would swing at. Mays hit everything between right-center field and left-center, but Hank used the whole field. He could put it down the foul lines."

Aaron was born on February 5, 1934, in a part of Mobile, Alabama, called Down by the Bay, a poor area of town populated mostly by blacks. The family moved to a better area of Mobile called Toulminville, where he was raised. That area also produced professional baseball players Satchel Paige, Willie McCovey, Billy Williams, Cleon Jones, Tommie Agee, Amos Otis, and Aaron's brother, Tommie.

One of six children born to Estella and Herbert Aaron, Hank grew up in a house his father built from lumber salvaged from a house that had been torn down. The meals came from their garden.

As a child and later as a teenager, Aaron's exposure to baseball began when major league teams would travel to Mobile during the spring-training exhibition season. He followed baseball closely and selected Joe DiMaggio, Jackie Robinson, and Stan Musial as his boyhood heroes.

Aaron actually began his own baseball career in an unorthodox manner. He was a cross-handed hitter, meaning he hit with his left hand over his right instead of the traditional way of right hand over left. Although his cross-handed batting technique should have reduced his power and was an invitation to broken wrists, he hit the ball hard enough to bat over .700 all the way through grammar school and high school.

"I probably should have become a switch-hitter. It would have been easy for me to move to the other side of the plate, where the left hand does belong over the right," Aaron said. "Instead, I learned to hold the bat properly while remaining a right-handed batter.

"Believe me, it was not easy."

Aaron also broke another one of the cardinal rules of hitting. He hit off his left foot. This was something that was never corrected because no coach—even when Aaron was a rookie—dared to change it. Normally, the action of hitting off a front foot would decrease the power of a hitter. But obviously, it had no effect on Aaron.

For the first two years of high school, Aaron played shortstop and third base for Central High School. He was the best player at the school, yet he still batted cross-handed. Aaron's team won the Negro high school championship of Mobile two years in a row and lost only three games. Aaron also played football for a year and was good enough to make All-City as a guard. But he gave up the sport after one year because he was frightened he would get hurt and ruin his baseball future.

For the final two years of high school, Aaron's parents sent him to Josephine Allen Institute, a private secondary school in Mobile. By this time, he was determined to be a professional baseball player. Aaron's parents did not approve of his dreams; they wanted him to finish school and go onto college.

When he was 15, Aaron played shortstop and third base for a semi-pro team called the Pritchett Athletics. It was the first time he had ever played a game of hardball. The team played mostly on Sundays, and Aaron was paid $3 a game.

Even at the tender age of 15, he showed more promise than any other player in Mobile. He joined the Mobile Black Bears, and by the time he was 17, he had become a star player. In a game against the highly successful Indianapolis Clowns, Aaron impressed with a double and two singles, and Syd Pollock, owner of the Clowns, sought to get Aaron for his team.

"I want that boy. But the first thing we must do is teach him to hold the bat properly," said Pollock. "I never saw anyone hit the ball so hard cross-handed."

But to get Aaron, the Clowns and Aaron had to get Aaron's mother to agree. She wanted her son to attend Florida A&M after high school, but the Clowns offered Hank $200 a month to play for them. Aaron's mother reached a compromise with her son and the Clowns. If he finished high school, he could sign with the Clowns.

Aaron agreed, and when he finished high school, he joined the Clowns. While playing for the Clowns, Aaron had four goals. The first one was to play in the big leagues; the second, to win an MVP; the third, to win a batting championship; and the fourth, to play in a World Series. He accomplished all of his goals in his baseball career.

The Milwaukee Braves heard about Aaron and sent a scout, Dewey Griggs, to observe the youngster. Griggs admired Aaron's skills, and eventually scouts, from the Yankees, Giants, and Phillies also were interested.

Aaron consulted with Pollock about his future, and the two agreed that the Braves and the Giants offered Aaron the best opportunity. Pollock left the final decision to Aaron, and he chose the Braves.

When Giants' manager Leo Durocher found out that the Giants had lost out to the Braves for Aaron's services, he was livid.

"How could we have lost that boy?" said Durocher. "We could have had him any number of times. Why, one of our scouts umpired a high school game he played in and never told us a word about him. And if what we offered to pay him wasn't enough, why didn't we go higher?"

The Braves assigned Aaron to the Eau Claire, Wisconsin, team in the

Class C Northern League and rushed him there directly from the Indianapolis Clowns. He got two hits in his first game and finished the season with a .336 batting average, nine home runs, and 61 RBI in only 87 games. He was a unanimous choice for Rookie of the Year.

In 1953, Aaron was promoted to the Jacksonville Tars of the Class A South Atlantic League, which was more commonly referred to as the Sally League. Aaron became the first black player in the Sally League and was one of three who entered the league that year.

Aaron won the Sally League's Most Valuable Player award in his first year with the Tars. He led the league in batting (.362), RBI (125), runs scored (115), hits (208), doubles (36), and total bases (338). He also was second in home runs with 22 and in triples with 14.

While he was in Jacksonville, he met and married Barbara Lucas. Hank and his new wife went to Puerto Rico the winter following their marriage so that Hank could play in the Puerto Rican Winter League. The manager, a former big leaguer named Mickey Owen, got Aaron to crouch in his stance at the plate. Now he was able to hit to all fields, where before he was mostly hitting to center and to left.

Owen also shifted Hank to the outfield at the request of the Braves' front office. Hank had never played anywhere but second base and shortstop, but he learned to play the outfield well in a very short time. After the Puerto Rican Winter League season was over, Owen told the Braves' front office that Hank was ready for the big leagues.

The Braves were not so sure. The Braves put him on their Triple A roster at the start of spring training, and he seemed ticketed for another year in the minors. But then one of the Braves' starting outfielders, Bobby Thomson, broke his ankle sliding into second base, and Aaron was promoted to take over the position.

On April 23, 1954, he got his first hit and, appropriately, it was a home run. Aaron spent most of the season as the Braves' regular left fielder but broke his ankle sliding on September 5 and was sidelined for the rest of the season. In 122 games, he batted .280 with 13 home runs. He would not hit below .280 again for a dozen years and not go below 20 homers for the next 20 years.

In 1955, Aaron moved to right field, where he remained for most of his career. He would win three Gold Gloves at the position. Aaron batted .314 with 27 homers and 106 RBI in 1955 and the next year won the first of his two NL batting titles with a .328 average.

Two things helped change Aaron into a more formidable run producer. In 1957, the Braves switched Aaron from second in the batting order to fourth, behind slugger Eddie Mathews instead of in front of him.

Aaron also switched from a 36-ounce bat to a 34-ounce model. He responded by leading the league with 44 homers and a career-high 132 RBI while batting .322.

In late September, Aaron hit an 11th-inning two-run homer off the Cardinals' Billy Muffett to clinch the Braves' first pennant in Milwaukee. His teammates carried him off the field, and Aaron has always maintained it was the best home run he ever hit.

The Braves went on to beat the New York Yankees in a seven-game World Series. While pitcher Lew Burdette won the Series MVP award by posting three victories, Aaron contributed mightily to the victory by batting .393 with three homers and seven RBI. Later that winter, the 23-year-old Aaron won the only MVP award of his career.

Aaron (.326, 30 homers, 95 RBI) led the Braves to another pennant in 1958, but this time the Braves lost a seven-game Series to the Yankees.

In 1959, Aaron won his second batting title (.355) and also led the league in hits (223) and slugging percentage (.636). The Braves finished in a tie for first place with the Los Angeles Dodgers but lost the pennant in a best-of-three playoff.

Aaron would never play on another pennant winner, although the 1969 Atlanta Braves would win the NL West title in the first year of divisional play. However, they were swept by the New York Mets in a best-of-five playoff.

As the years went on, Aaron continued to compile some impressive statistics. From 1960 to 1967, he won three more home run titles and three RBI titles. After the 1971 season, it became apparent that Aaron had a legitimate chance to beat Ruth's record.

He had two things going for him: playing home games in a good hitter's ballpark and those powerful wrists and forearms. Aaron hit 34 homers in only 129 games in 1972 and belted 40 in just 120 games in 1973, finishing the season only one home run short of Ruth.

Aaron tied Ruth's record on April 4, 1974, hitting a three-run homer off Billingham on his first at-bat of the season. Baseball commissioner Bowie Kuhn and Vice President Gerald Ford congratulated him on the field, and the game was held up for six minutes.

"I'm not embarrassed at all," said Billingham. "He deserved it. He's the greatest I've ever seen."

After Aaron connected off Downing four days later, pandemonium erupted throughout the ballpark. Downing had been a teammate of Roger Maris when he broke Ruth's single-season record in 1961, but he said far more excitement greeted Aaron's blast.

"The game literally stopped," Downing said. "A ceremony had been scripted. They had a half-hour show with [entertainer] Sammy Davis Jr. on the field. When Maris hit his homer, we had to push him on the field for a curtain call, and that was it."

President Richard Nixon phoned congratulations to Aaron during the game, and Claire Ruth, Babe's widow, sent Hank a congratulatory wire. "I know the Babe was pulling for Hank," she said.

Aaron's feelings were sighs of relief.

"I just thank God it's over," Aaron said.

The 1974 season marked Hank's final one with the Braves. He returned to Milwaukee, the city of his fondest memories, and served as a designated hitter with the Brewers for two more seasons. He hit 22 more home runs before calling it quits after the 1976 campaign.

After retiring as a player, Aaron became one of the first blacks in major league baseball's upper-level management. He returned to the Braves as Atlanta's vice president of player development, then later became a senior vice president. He also served for Turner Broadcasting as a corporate vice president of community relations and a member of TBS's board of directors.

Stan Musial

Ranking: 4th
Hit Total: 3,630

AP/Wide World Photos

Stan Musial was in terrible pain. Both his wrists were aching so badly that he could hardly grip a bat. He had injured his left one making a diving catch five days earlier, and the right one had been plunked by Brooklyn's Carl Erskine only the previous day. Each swing he took made the St. Louis Cardinals' outfielder grimace.

"I don't know if I'll be able to do much," he told manager Eddie Dyer, "but I'll give it a try."

Stan felt it was his duty to play. After all, the Cardinals' opponents on this late summer day in 1948 were the Boston Braves, and they were on an eight-game winning streak and in the thick of the National League pennant race.

Doc Weaver, the Cardinals' trainer, thought he'd found a solution to ease the pain in Musial's wrists. He bandaged them tightly, but this caused Stan to lose the snap in his swing, and so he ripped them off right before the game began.

Musial stepped to the plate in the first inning against Braves left-hander Warren Spahn, one of the best pitchers in the game. He knew that with his bad wrists, he would not be able to pull the ball off Spahn, so he looped a single to left on the first pitch.

In Musial's next at-bat, Spahn's first pitch was a high fastball on the outside part of the plate, and the Cardinals' slugger flicked his bat out quickly and laced it over the left-fielder's head for a double.

By the time Musial strode to the plate in the fourth inning, the Braves had replaced Spahn with Red Barrett. He fed Musial a change-up on the first pitch, and the Cardinals' slugger swung from the heels, his wrists throbbing as he started his swing. The bat met the ball solidly and the ball landed in the right-field bullpen for Musial's 38th home run of the year.

Musial's wrists were burning with pain when he strode to the plate in the sixth against reliever Clyde Shoun. On Shoun's first pitch, Musial poked a *pitch past shortstop Alvin Dark for a single, his fourth straight hit.*

Al Lyons, a wild, young right-hander, was the Braves' pitcher in the eighth, and he went to 2-0 on Musial. The Cardinals' bench began hollering at Lyons to throw strikes, and when the next pitch was near the strike zone, Musial swung and hit a grounder between first and second base that rolled into right field for a single.

It marked the fourth time in the season that Musial had managed five hits in a game, tying a record set by Ty Cobb. What was remarkable about Musial's achievement, however, was that the hits came on just five swings.

"The pain in my wrists was so intense that I'd made up my mind I wasn't going to waste any swings," Musial recalled. "I knew I couldn't do much swinging, anyway. In other words, the five hits I made that afternoon were the only swings I took all afternoon. I didn't miss any, I didn't foul any. I swung five times and got five hits."

Such was the virtuosity of Stan Musial, a hitter held in such high esteem that he was known simply as "The Man."

Stanley Frank Musial was the most popular player ever to wear a Cardinals' uniform. An outfielder/first baseman, he had an unorthodox batting stance with his feet close together and his body coiled at the plate like a human corkscrew.

"He looks, as he stands up there, like a kid peeking around the corner to see if the cops are coming," said pitcher Ted Lyons.

But, while he may have looked uncomfortable, Musial ranks among the best hitters of all time. He played 22 years (1941-63) for the Cardinals and amassed 3,630 hits while compiling a lifetime batting average of .331. He led the NL in batting seven times, knocked in 100 or more runs 10 times, and scored 100 or more runs 11 times.

He also led the league in doubles eight times, in triples five times, and in slugging percentage six times. Although he never led the league in home runs, he did top the 30 mark six times and finished his career with 475.

He was named the NL's Most Valuable Player in 1941, 1946, and 1948.

Musial was such a good hitter that he went through 17 consecutive seasons before his average dipped below .310. He had such great charisma that he was elected to play in 24 All-Star Games. In the late 1940s, a song was even written about him, extolling his exploits on the baseball diamond.

Yet he might never have achieved such fame if it hadn't been for an injury he suffered that ruined his career as a left-handed pitcher. In 1940, while playing in the minor leagues during his third season of professional baseball, Stan injured his shoulder while attempting a shoestring catch in the outfield. The injury ended his career as a pitcher but led to a career as a dominant hitter.

Born on November 21, 1920, Musial was the fifth of six children born to Polish miner Lukasz Musial and Czech American Mary Lancos. A basketball and baseball star at Donora High School, Musial was offered a basketball scholarship to Duquesne University in Pittsburgh, but turned it down because he wanted to play professional baseball.

He began his baseball career as a pitcher and once struck out 17 batters in a seven-inning high school game. When not pitching, he played the outfield and drew more attention by belting a 450-foot homer while playing for an amateur team in Donora.

The Cleveland Indians and the New York Yankees expressed interest in the 6-foot, 180-pound left-hander, but the Cardinals showed the most interest and signed Stan in 1938 for their minor league organization.

He went 6-6 for West Virginia of the Mountain States League in his first season of pro ball in 1938 and was 9-2 the next year, when he developed a sore arm. The Cardinals sent him to Daytona Beach of the Florida State League under the guidance of Dickie Kerr, a former star pitcher for the Chicago White Sox. Kerr took an immediate liking to Musial. Upon learning that Stan's wife was pregnant and the young couple was having trouble making ends meet, Kerr invited the Musials to live with him and his wife. The Musials named their first son Richard in honor of Kerr.

Years later, Musial would repay Kerr's kindness even more. When he began to make big money for the Cardinals, Musial secretly bought a house for Kerr and his wife in Houston, Texas. He presented it to them for their help and friendship.

In 1940, his first year under Kerr's tutelage, Musial went 18-5 as a pitcher, but on August 13, his whole world collapsed around him.

"We were playing at Orlando," Stan recalled. "I think we were a run ahead, but Orlando had men on first and second with two out. The batter hit a low liner toward me in center, and I came in fast, trying for a shoestring catch. Just as I lunged for the ball, my spikes caught in the turf. I fell, landing heavily on my left shoulder. I dropped the ball, two runs scored, and we lost the game.

"The pain was terrific. They had to help me off the field. The docs said it was only a dislocation, but I couldn't throw for two weeks. A week after that, I tried to take my turn pitching. I managed to last the nine innings, but I couldn't throw anything but soft stuff. Four days later, against Orlando, I could hardly reach the plate. They knocked me out in the first inning. As a pitcher I was through. I knew it. It was a desperate time.

With his wife, Lillian, expecting the couple's first child, Stan thought about quitting baseball. Kerr talked him out of it.

"You can't quit. You're big league," Kerr told Stan. "You can't miss. You're a fine all-around player and one hell of a hitter."

Musial wasn't sure, but he decided to give it one more try as an outfielder. The next spring he reported to Columbus, Georgia, to train with the Cardinals' Class C and D clubs. His shoulder felt better, but he still couldn't pitch. One day, Branch Rickey, the head of the Cardinals' farm system, came to camp. He watched Stan take batting practice, then called the youngster aside.

"I've seen you hit, and I'm going to make an outfielder of you," he told Musial. "I doubt whether you'd ever have become a big-league pitcher, even if you hadn't hurt your arm."

Given hope by Rickey's confidence in him, Musial went to the Cardinals' Springfield, Missouri, club in the Western Association. He hit .389 and belted a league-leading 26 homers in only 87 games. In mid-season, he was promoted to Rochester of the International League. He was equally impressive there, batting .326 with the AAA team in 54 games. He was called up to the Cardinals at the end of the season and hit .426 in 12 games.

Musial's performance so impressed manager Billy Southworth that he promised Stan a starting job for the next season. Southworth kept his word, and Stan was the starting left fielder for the 1942 season. Musial hit .315 in his rookie year as the Cardinals won the NL pennant and beat the New York Yankees in a five-game World Series.

In 1943, Stan batted .357 to win the first of his seven batting titles. He also led the league in hits, doubles, and triples to earn MVP honors and help the Cardinals to their second straight pennant. The Yankees, however, reversed their World Series loss of the previous season and won in five games.

With Musial leading the league in hits and batting .347, the Cardinals won the pennant for the third year in a row in 1944 and beat the crosstown rival St. Louis Browns in the World Series. Musial went into the Navy in 1945 and was stationed with a ship-repairing unit. He was able to work on his hitting a little, but his absence, along with that of several other prominent members of the team, probably cost the Cardinals their fourth straight pennant. Instead, the Chicago Cubs emerged as NL champions.

Musial returned to civilian life in 1946, and the Cardinals returned to the top of the NL. Playing first base for the entire season, Stan hit .365 to win his second batting crown and also led the league in hits, runs, doubles, and triples. He was named the MVP for the second time. The Cardinals won their third World Series in five years by beating the Boston Red Sox in seven games.

In 1946, several major leaguers left to play in Mexico for higher wages. Musial was courted heavily by Jorge Pasquel, the president of the Mexican League. Musial refused to leave the Cardinals, and that helped stem the tide of Pasquel's raids.

Although Stan never had a serious injury during his major league career, he did experience an illness in the 1947 season, and it caused his average to slip to .250 for most of the season, until Musial finished at .312.

"They tell me I hit about .480 the last two months," he said. "I had to reach that .300 mark. I think I finally pulled myself up to .300 around the beginning of September. I had five hits in six times at bat against Chicago."

Stan's best season came in 1948. That year he hit a career-high .376 and led the NL in batting, hits, runs, doubles, triples, slugging percentage, and RBI. He won the MVP for the third time. It was also the year in which he earned the nickname "The Man."

Many recall that it happened one night at Brooklyn's Ebbets Field. Musial had been ripping Dodger pitching all night, and when he strode to the plate in the top of the ninth, some of the 32,888 fans began to chant in unison, "Oooh, ooh, here comes the man again. Here comes the man." The nickname stuck. Musial then singled for his fifth hit of the night and later scored his fifth run as the Cardinals walloped the Dodgers, 14-7.

Musial had five hits that night and 11 hits in 15 at-bats, including four doubles, a triple, and a homer, in the three-game series. A year later he would hit over .500 against Brooklyn pitching.

From 1949 through 1957, Stan's batting average was never lower than .330, and there was only one season in which he drove in fewer than 100 runs. On May 2, 1954, he had one of the greatest days of his career, hitting five home runs in a doubleheader against the New York Giants. He ranked that day as the best of his career.

"After I hit my fourth home run, the public address announcer said I'd just tied a record," said Musial. "Up to then, I hadn't been paying any attention to my homers. I'd just met the ball solidly four times, and it went all the way.

"That's when I determined to try for a fifth homer. Hoyt Wilhelm was pitching, and I'd never hit him particularly well. He threw me a knuckler and—oh, boy—that fifth homer was the best shot of them all. It went all the way over the roof in right-center."

Musial's career was remarkably consistent. He was the first player to appear in 1,000 games at two positions, and he maintained a career average higher than .323 in every month of the season. He also managed the odd feat of dividing his 3,630 lifetime hits evenly between 1,815 at home and 1,815 on the road.

In 1958, Musial reached the 3,000-hit club. The historic hit came as a pinch hitter at Chicago's Wrigley Field late in the season. Cardinals manager Fred Hutchinson told Musial he wanted Stan to get the 3,000th hit at home the next day and would use him in the game only if necessary.

The Cards were behind, 3-1, going into the sixth inning when they got a man on base against young pitcher Moe Drabowsky. Hutchinson then signaled for Musial to pinch-hit. Drabowsky delivered a breaking pitch, and Musial laced it for a double to reach the milestone.

Musial's playing time began to dwindle after the 1958 season, although he hung around for five more years. After hitting .337 in 1958, he slumped to .255 in 115 games in 1959. He followed that with another subpar .275 campaign in 1960 and batted .288 in 1961.

He rebounded in 1962 to hit .330 in 135 games, but team adviser Branch Rickey started a controversy by suggesting that Musial's comeback that year at the age of 42 was his last hurrah and that he should retire. The Cardinals' front office did not like Rickey's suggestion, and Musial was embarrassed by the commotion caused by the controversy. However, Rickey proved to be right, as Musial faded to .255 in 1963, then announced his retirement.

Few players in history were held in such high esteem by their peers. "Stash," as he was known to his teammates, was among the best-liked and most-respected players in baseball. Teammates, baseball writers, rival players, and umpires all had the same affection for him.

After his retirement, Musial opened a restaurant in St. Louis and got involved in banking and other businesses. He also became an accomplished harmonica player and wrote a book on how to play the instrument.

The Cardinals also found a place for him in the front office as a senior vice president, but in 1967 he was asked to take over for Bob Howsam as the team's general manager at the urging of field manager and former roommate Red Schoendienst.

Musial proved to be as adept as a general manager as he was as a player. He helped guide the Cardinals to the world championship in 1967, then abruptly quit as GM to devote his time to his other businesses.

In 1969, he was elected to the Hall of Fame on the first ballot.

Tris Speaker

Ranking: 5th
Hit Total: 3,514

SPI Archives

The Cleveland Indians were badly in need of a lift. They were battling the Chicago White Sox and New York Yankees for the 1920 pennant, but the Indians' spirits were down. Their short-stop, Ray Chapman, had been killed by a pitched ball thrown by New York's Carl Mays a short time earlier, and the club was understandably despondent.

Even manager Tris Speaker, the Indians' star center fielder, admitted to having "lost some taste" for the pennant run.

But with the pennant race winding down, the team was in a crucial September game with the White Sox. The White Sox had loaded the bases with two outs late in the game, and Joe Jackson, one of the most dangerous hitters in the league, stepped to the plate.

Jackson hit a savage line drive to right-center that looked as if it would be a certain triple. Speaker turned at the crack of the bat and took off like a jackrabbit toward right-center field. Even for the best center fielder in the game, the possibility of catching the ball seemed remote.

But Speaker was not about to give up on it. He streaked toward the exit gate, only to arrive just at about the time the ball was descending from its flight. With a perfectly timed jump, he leaped in the air with both feet off the ground, snared the ball in his glove, and crashed against the concrete wall. He fell to the ground and lay unconscious for several minutes. When the players finally got to Speaker, he still had the ball in his glove. It had to be pried loose.

The catch, which many consider the greatest he ever made, saved the game and, most likely, the pennant for the Indians. They went on to win the American League flag and defeat the Brooklyn Dodgers in the World Series.

Dogged determination. That was a trademark of Tris Speaker, who prac-tically revolutionized outfield play during his 22 years in the major leagues, as well as recording 3,515 hits and a lifetime batting average of .344.

That determination was never more evident than in the 1912 World Series, when he delivered the decisive game-winning hit in the 10th inning of Game 7 to give the Boston Red Sox the championship.

The Red Sox and New York Giants were deadlocked at three games apiece, and Giants ace pitcher Christy Mathewson seemed to have the Series locked up when the Giants took a 2-1 lead in the 10th inning.

But the Red Sox got a break in their half of the 10th when pinch hitter Clyde Engle's low line drive was dropped in center field by Fred Snodgrass. After Harry Hooper flied out, Mathewson walked Steve Yerkes, and Speaker stepped to the plate.

Speaker, known as "Spoke" to his teammates, always felt he could hit the great Mathewson, but this time he lofted a high foul between home plate and first base. It appeared to be an easy play for Giants first baseman Fred Merkle. Speaker knew that catcher Chief Meyers would have a tough time catching the ball and was just about to yell out his name when he heard Mathewson yell, "Meyers, Meyers."

Speaker was right all along. Meyers couldn't catch up to it, as the wind was blowing the ball away. At the last second, Merkle made a lunging attempt for the ball, but it fell to the ground. Given a reprieve, Speaker yelled at Mathewson, "You just blew the championship, Matty."

Spoke was true to his word. On the next pitch, he singled to right, scoring Engle with the tying run. After Duffy Lewis drew another walk to load the bases, Larry Gardner hit a sacrifice fly that gave the Red Sox a 3-2 victory and the world championship.

Never give a superstar a second chance.

Tris Speaker was as tough as they came, both mentally and physically, whether it was coming through in the clutch during a game or battling with owners over a contract. He was hard-nosed and hardheaded and, quite possibly, the greatest center fielder who ever played the game.

He is credited with revolutionizing outfield play. He was the first to "read" a batter and position himself from left to right as the pitch was on its way to the plate. He played so shallow in center field that he was known as the "fifth infielder," but he had uncanny ability to go back on any ball hit over his head.

Speaker's shallow outfield positioning enabled him to record four unassisted double plays during his career. He also was able to take pickoff throws at second base from the pitcher and catcher, throw batters out on balls hit up the middle, and even turn the pivot on a double play.

Known as "The Gray Eagle" because of his prematurely gray hair and his knack for swooping balls out of the air, Speaker led outfielders in putouts seven times, in assists three times, in double plays five times, and in fielding average twice. His 448 outfield assists are the most ever recorded.

As a hitter, he was second only to Ty Cobb during his era. He had more doubles (792) than any player, 200 or more hits in a season four times, and batted .300 or better in 18 seasons. A left-handed hitter who held the bat near his hip and with his hands spread about three inches apart, Speaker won the AL batting title in 1916 with a .386 average, the only year Cobb did not win it from 1907 to 1919. At one time or another, he led the league in hits (twice), doubles (eight times), home runs (once), RBI (once), and slugging average (once). He also hit 11 or more triples in a season 13 times, scored 100 or more runs seven times, and had 30 or more stolen bases seven times.

As great as Speaker was, no superstar of baseball probably ever had more trouble convincing people that he could play. As a youngster, he was turned down by the Red Sox, Pittsburgh, and the New York Giants before finally getting a second chance with Boston and making the grade.

Born in Hubbard, Texas, on April 4, 1888, Tristam E. Speaker learned about doing things the hard way from a very early age. He was one of eight children, six of them girls, born to parents of English stock, but when Tris was only 10, his father died, leaving him and his brother as the breadwinners.

Tris was close to his mother, but she had trouble keeping up with the high-spirited youngster who loved to ride equally high-spirited horses.

When Tris was very young, he twice broke his right arm in falls from horses, and as a result, he began to throw left-handed when his love turned to baseball.

At the age of 17, he enrolled at Fort Worth Polytechnic Institute in hopes of becoming an engineer. He soon found he loved baseball more than mathematics. He pitched for the school team, then picked up some money hurling for the Nicholson and Watson semipro team of Corsicana, Texas. He also worked as a telegraph lineman and a cowboy to earn extra money.

Speaker eventually landed a job pitching for a professional team in Cleburne, Texas, but it didn't take long for the manager to realize that pitching was not the youngster's forte. In one game, Speaker was tagged for 22 runs, and the Cleburne manager, Benny Shelton, did not know what to do with him.

"Put me in right field," Tris said. "I'm the best right fielder in the league."

Shelton glared at the youngster but put him in the outfield, and he was there to stay.

A year later, when Roberts transferred his Cleburne franchise to Houston and the Texas League, Speaker hit .315 and stole 36 bases in 118 games. Jim McAleer, manager of the St. Louis Browns, had been impressed by Speaker in exhibition games and asked Roberts to wire him when he thought the youngster was ready to play.

Roberts sent McAleer two wires at mid-season, but both went unanswered. He tried one more time, sending the following message:

"SPEAKER READY. YOU CAN HAVE HIM FOR $1,500. I OWN 200 ACRES GOOD TEXAS BLACK LAND. WILL DEED TO YOU IF SPEAKER DOES NOT MAKE GOOD."

When McAleer still did not answer, Roberts sold Speaker to the Red Sox for $750.

Speaker was hardly an immediate hit with Boston. He joined the club in September of 1907 and managed only three hits in 19 at-bats. The Red Sox thought so little of him that they failed to send him a contract the following spring.

But Speaker remained undaunted at the Red Sox rejection. Now a free agent, he traveled to the Giants' spring training camp at Marlin, Texas, to try to sell himself to manager John McGraw.

"I begged him for a chance, but he already had more players at the camp than he knew what to do with," Speaker recalled in his later years.

Turned down by McGraw, Speaker wired other major league clubs about his availability. A Pittsburgh scout was interested, but Pirates owner

Barney Dreyfuss wanted no part of Speaker because he smoked.

Eventually, Speaker went to Little Rock, Arkansas, where the Red Sox were doing their 1908 training. The Red Sox agreed to let him work out with the club, but when the players broke camp, they left Speaker behind. The Red Sox were hurting for cash and couldn't pay their rent for the spring training facilities. They asked the owner of the Little Rock club, Mickey Finn, if he would accept Speaker instead.

Finn agreed. The Red Sox let Finn have Speaker with the agreement that he would give them first right to reacquire the youngster for $500.

Finn was a very knowledgeable baseball man and had a knack with young players. Under his guidance, Speaker proceeded to dominate the Southern League. He hit .350, the highest average in the league up to that time, and he stole 28 bases. Suddenly, teams that had shunned him now were interested.

True to his word, Finn sold Speaker back to the Red Sox for $500. He batted only .220 in 31 games, but he fielded his position so brilliantly that the Red Sox tabbed him as their starting center fielder for the 1909 season.

He hit .309 in his first season with the Red Sox, and the next year, a new manager, Patsy Donovan, surrounded him in the outfield with George "Duffy" Lewis in left and Harry Hooper in right. The trio became known as one of the best outfields ever assembled, and in 1912, with first baseman Jake Stahl as the manager, helped bring Boston the world championship.

Tris was voted the Most Valuable Player in the league that year. He batted .383, scored 136 runs, stole 52 bases, and led the league in doubles (53) and outfield assists (35).

Speaker's outfield play was sharpened by some helpful assistance he got from Cy Young, the famous pitcher who was with the Red Sox when Speaker broke into the big leagues.

"Cy was a veteran near the end of his playing career around the time I got my big-league start in Boston," Speaker once remarked. "The old fellow took a fancy to me and said he'd help make a slick outfielder out of me. He'd take me out on the practice field and hit fungoes to me by the hour. I got to watching and studying his fungo swing, and by doing that, I could start after the ball before he actually hit it.

"It later served a good purpose when I started playing regularly in center field. By closely observing the batsman at the plate, after he had reached a certain arc in his batting swing, I knew whether the ball would go to the right or left, and I also could gauge the power of the swing. In that way, I got the jump on the ball."

No outfielder ever played as shallow a center field as Speaker. Baseball was still in the dead-ball era when he began playing professionally, and he reasoned that few, if any, balls would be hit over his head. If they were, he had faith in his ability to go back and catch them.

"I once figured out that 98 percent of all safe hits to the outfield drop in front of the fielders," he said. "Only two percent go over their heads or between them. It really was confidence in these percentages that made me play so close in."

Following their 1912 championship season, the Red Sox were beaten out by the Philadelphia Athletics the next two years despite Speaker's inspired play. Then, in 1915, Boston won another world championship. Speaker hit .322 that season and batted .294 in the World Series as the Red Sox defeated the Philadelphia Phillies in five games.

Less than a year later, however, Speaker would be traded to the Cleveland Indians in a deal that ranks among the worst baseball trades ever made.

Speaker's relationship with the Red Sox began to sour in the winter of 1915, after Boston owner Joe Lannin tried to reduce his salary. Lannin had been irked at Speaker for entertaining offers from the new Federal League prior to the 1914 season, and with the Federal League now out of business, the Red Sox owner was determined to bring down his payroll.

Lannin had paid Speaker $18,000 for the 1915 season, but now he wanted to slice it in half. Speaker, expecting a raise, was furious. He refused to play for anything less than $15,000.

Manager Bill Carrigan was caught in the middle, but he convinced Lannin to allow Speaker to go to spring training to Little Rock, Arkansas, and play in exhibition games for a fixed fee. Carrigan figured the two men would reach a compromise, and at least his star player would be in shape.

Speaker agreed to the arrangement, but he was still unsigned as the exhibition season was to get under way.

The newspapers were writing daily about the feud brewing between Lannin and Speaker, and Ed Bang, the sports editor of the Cleveland paper, showed a clipping of the story to Jimmy Dunn, the president of the Cleveland Indians.

"I think Tris can be bought if you go after Lannin in the right way," Bang suggested. Dunn immediately took a train to Boston to meet with Lannin.

Speaker, meanwhile, was having a great spring. In the final game of the exhibition season against the Dodgers at Ebbets Field, Speaker hit a game-winning homer off Rube Marquard. He was given assurances by

Lannin that he would be signed by opening day, which was only two days away.

Hours later, Speaker was packing in his hotel for the trip to Boston when he received a phone call from the lobby from Bob McRoy, the Indians' general manager, who wanted to talk to him.

Puzzled, Speaker invited McRoy up to the room, where they talked generalities before McRoy got to the point of the meeting: "How would you like to play for Cleveland, Tris?"

"I wouldn't," Tris replied. "You've not only got a bad ball club, but you've got a bad baseball town."

McRoy hesitated for a moment. "I wish," he said, "you didn't feel that way. We've made a deal for you."

Tris protested, but the deal had already been announced. He had been traded for pitcher Sam Jones, infielder Fred Thomas, and $50,000.

Speaker informed McRoy that he would go to Cleveland only if he got $10,000 of the purchase price. When Tris threatened to go home to Texas, Fannin came through with the money.

While Boston was still good enough to win the World Series in 1916, Speaker revitalized baseball in Cleveland. In his first season with the Indians, he hit .386 to beat out Cobb for the batting title. Three years later, he was made player/manager, and in 1920 he led the Indians to the world championship.

Speaker remained one of the league's big stars and served as player/manager of the Indians until 1926. Several weeks after the close of the 1926 season, Cleveland fans were stunned to read that Speaker had resigned to go into business in Cleveland about the same time Cobb resigned as player/manager in Detroit.

Then news broke that Hubert "Dutch" Leonard, a pitcher who had been a teammate of Speaker's in Boston and had played for Cobb in Detroit, accused the two superstars of conspiring to fix a late-season game during the 1919 season. Ban Johnson, the American League president, forced Speaker and Cobb to resign.

With both men protesting their innocence, baseball commissioner Kennesaw Mountain Landis launched an investigation that cleared the two men. They were reinstated and ordered to finish their careers in the American League. Speaker played for Washington in 1927, batted .327 in 141 games, and closed his career as a member of the Athletics in 1928. He and Cobb were teammates on the A's 1928 club, though their skills had eroded considerably.

Speaker managed the Newark Bears of the International League in 1929, and in 1930 he became a broadcaster for Cubs and White Sox games in Chicago. He tried his hand at owning a minor league team in Kansas City, but when that failed, he returned to Cleveland briefly as a broadcaster. In Cleveland, he became associated with a wholesale liquor business and prospered representing a Detroit steel firm.

In 1937, Speaker was voted into the Hall of Fame, and 10 years later, he helped launch the career of another Cleveland Hall of Famer, Larry Doby, by helping convert the young infielder into a center fielder. Under Speaker's tutelage, Doby, the first black player in the American League, became one of the best center fielders of his era.

Cap Anson

Ranking: 6th
Hit Total: 3,435

AP/Wide World Photos

Thehe stands began to fill early at Toledo's League Park on August 10, 1883. The local team, known as the Toledos, was one of the best minor league clubs of the era, and its opponent on this Friday afternoon was the three-time world-champion Chicago White Stockings, led by their star player/manager, Cap Anson.

It was customary in those days for major league teams to schedule exhibition games on their days off against the better minor league teams, and thousands of fans turned out for a chance to see the world champions in action.

What happened on that warm summer day would have an adverse effect on baseball for more than 60 years—and Cap Anson would be the antagonist.

Anson was a big man, both in physical stature and in the prestige he carried throughout baseball. In size, Anson was an imposing figure, standing six feet tall and weighing 227 pounds. He was handsome, sported a black handlebar mustache, and spurned alcohol and tobacco, unlike most of the other players of his day.

Known for his shrewd maneuvers on the ball field, as well as for his ability with a bat in his hands, Anson was looked up to by virtually everyone in baseball.

But he also was loud, belligerent, and foulmouthed. He refined umpire intimidation to a science. And there was another ugly side to Anson that would erupt on this day in Toledo and shake the very foundations of the game.

One of the players on the Toledo team that day was Moses Fleetwood "Fleet" Walker, a former Oberlin College student who was playing baseball to earn money for law school at the University of Michigan. A fair-hitting, good-fielding catcher/outfielder, Walker was the offspring of an interracial marriage. One of his parents was black, making him one of the few black players in organized baseball at the time.

Walker had earned respect for his play and his hard work on and off the field. He was heralded as "a gentleman and a scholar," yet his mere presence on the ball field did not sit well with Anson.

Anson had made it known to the Toledo management that he objected to playing on the same field with blacks, and the Toledos planned on going along with Anson by benching Walker, who was suffering from a sore hand and was unable to catch, anyway.

When the White Stockings arrived at Union Station on Friday morning, they were informed that Walker would be kept on the bench. However, that was not good enough for Anson, who demanded that Walker be told to leave the stadium.

Anson's attitude offended Toledo manager Charles Morton. He promptly inserted Walker into the lineup in right field. When Anson saw Walker in right field, he exploded. Screaming at the top of his lungs, Anson ordered Morton to get Walker off the field or he would take his team back to Chicago.

When Morton informed Anson that not playing the game would result in the forfeiture of all box-office receipts, Anson relented. However, he made it clear that his team would never again play against a team with a black man in the lineup.

The exhibition game played in Toledo turned out to be one of the most important games in baseball history. From this game came the impetus for the systematic exclusion of blacks from the game, a ban that would last for 63 years—until Jackie Robinson broke the color barrier with the Brooklyn Dodgers in 1947.

Although there was no official color line in professional baseball in the 1880s, it was only 18 years after the Civil War had ended, and America still struggled with the placement of newly freed blacks in society. The cries grew louder that blacks did not belong on the same playing fields as whites. Blacks

also began to find theaters, restaurants, transportation, union shops, and skilled

vocations closed to them. Jim Crow laws and the Ku Klux Klan became more

prominent in American political life.

Anson jumped into this controversy with both feet.

Adrian Constantine Anson, a man named after two Roman emperors, was a dominant name in baseball for three decades. As "Baby" Anson, he became a star as a teenager in 1871 and moved to Chicago when the National League was formed in 1876.

As "Cap" Anson, he became player/manager of the White Stockings in 1879 and held the post until, as "Pop" Anson, he retired as both player and manager in 1897.

A right-handed batter with a split batting grip, he compiled a .329 career batting average over 27 seasons and won four batting championships. He averaged an RBI every five at-bats and was the first major leaguer to reach 3,000 hits (in comparatively short seasons).

Anson was incredibly durable, serving as a regular for all 22 of his National League seasons in addition to his five in the National Association. He is the second-oldest major leaguer to hit a grand slam, delivering his clout in July of 1894 at the age of 42, and the second-oldest—at age 45—to hit a home run at all, connecting for two on October 3, 1897, the last day of his career.

In addition, he excelled as a manager, compiling a .632 won-lost percentage during the 1880s and winning five pennants.

Anson is generally considered the greatest baseball player of the 19th century and in 1939 was among the fourth group inducted into the Hall of Fame.

Unfortunately, Cap Anson was also a world-class racist. He firmly believed that blacks were inferior to whites and he made no secret about his feelings. What was even more unfortunate was that a lot of people listened to Cap Anson, the towering figure of baseball in the 1880s.

The game in Toledo attracted national attention and crystallized the segregation forces already at work in professional baseball. In time, more teams and leagues began to release black players and refused to hire new ones. The Toledos joined the American Association in 1884, making Fleet Walker the first black major leaguer. His brother, Welday, played five games for Toledo and became the second.

Anson and his White Stockings returned to Toledo for another exhibition on July 25, 1884, but this time controversy was avoided. Both Walker brothers, by prior agreement, stayed on the bench.

However, things continued to go poorly for Fleet Walker. He was booed and hissed at a game in Louisville, Kentucky, in early May, and in Richmond, Virginia, later in the season. He also had trouble with Tony Mullane, one of the great pitchers of the era. Mullane disliked blacks and would throw anything he pleased at the plate, never letting his catcher, Walker, know what pitch was coming. As a result, Walker was charged with several passed balls every time he caught Mullane.

Walker batted .263 for the 1884 season, but his sore hands caused his release on September 23, 1884. No black man would play in the major leagues again until Robinson joined the Dodgers in 1947.

Walker played for minor league teams in Cleveland, Newark, and other cities for several more years, and he crossed paths with Anson again. In 1887, Anson threatened to cancel an exhibition against the Newark team rather than face the black star of the team, pitcher George Stovey. Stovey and his catcher, Fleet Walker, both remained on the bench for the duration of the game.

Anson's campaign began to have an effect. After the season, Newark released Stovey despite his 33 wins. By 1889, Walker was the only black remaining in the high minor leagues, and soon after, the color line was firmly in place throughout professional baseball.

Walker turned to political pursuits, editing a newspaper with his brother, Welday, and advocating black resettlement in Africa. He died in Cleveland in 1924 and was buried in an unmarked grave.

Anson, meanwhile, went on to a glorious career in baseball. A hard-driving disciplinarian, he was perhaps the most influential player in the 19th century. He played in the first professional league, the National Association, from its inception in 1871 and hit .331 in the National League 25 years later.

Anson's White Stockings became known as the Colts and then the Cubs, the name they bear today. Anson is still the Cubs' all-time leader in hits, runs batted in, and batting average.

As a baseball innovator, he had few equals. He was the first manager to rotate pitchers, the first to use signals to his hitters and fielders, the first to use the platoon system, and the first to conduct a preseason spring-training camp. In addition, he is credited by many with inventing the hit-

and-run play.

The exchange of lineup cards before games also is a direct result of Anson's managerial genius. Until the league made that practice mandatory, Anson would send to the plate two batters of his choice to open the game. If either got into scoring position, Anson would bat third, figuring his productive bat had an excellent chance of driving in a run. If neither batter got to second base, he would send another player to bat and save himself for a more opportune moment to hit.

He also was a nemesis for umpires and was fined repeatedly by umpires and baseball officials. He earned the nickname "Baby" (for crybaby) before cleaning up his act.

As a manager, he would fine players for being overweight, for drinking, and for missing curfews. He used bed checks to keep tabs on his players but also got them first-class hotel rooms and personally marched them onto the field single file before every game.

Rigid in his discipline, he would even bar team owner Albert Spalding from the clubhouse if he deemed it necessary, and he sometimes was forced to enforce his rules with his fists.

Anson also was a clever promoter. He often dressed his players in costumes from Native American dress to formal wear and paraded them through the streets of National League cities in open carriages to irritate local fans and stimulate them to buy tickets to the day's game.

It all began for Anson in the town of Marshalltown, Iowa, where he grew up among the Pottawattamie Indians. He and his brother, Sturgis, began playing "base ball" (it didn't become one word until much later) at a young age, and they are credited with introducing the sport to the University of Notre Dame in 1866.

After a year at Notre Dame, Anson turned pro with the National Association's Rockford Forest Citys. He went from there to the Philadelphia Athletics, for whom he played third base for four years. He joined Chicago when White Stockings owner William Hulbert formed the National League.

Originally used primarily as a catcher and an outfielder for Chicago, he moved to first base in 1879 and stayed at that position for the rest of his career. He also became the team's captain, the equivalent of player/manager, in 1879. That earned him the nickname "Cap," for which he was known for most of his career.

As he continued playing well into his 40s, he became known as "Pop." A poor fielder with little mobility, Anson was an outstanding hitter. In addition to winning four batting titles, he won the RBI crown nine times from 1880 to 1891.

His highest single-season batting average was .421 in 1887, but that mark was padded because walks counted as hits that season. Nevertheless, that season aside, Anson's lifetime hit total is remarkable since pitchers of his era usually threw from 10 to 15 feet closer than they do today.

"When I broke in with the White Stockings in 1876, pitchers then were allowed seven to nine balls, delivered the ball from only 45 then 50 feet and pitched in a box six to seven feet long—not from a slab—and could take a run when delivering the ball," Anson once told a reporter.

As a manager, he led Chicago to pennants in 1880, 1881, 1882, 1885, and 1886. Following the 1885 season, Anson decided to do something about the physical conditioning of his players. Since many were in the habit of reporting for the start of the season badly out of shape, Anson ordered his players to report to Hot Springs, Arkansas, to "boil out" almost two months before the season started.

Hot Springs was a celebrated spa. Though the town's population was only about 10,000, there were always between 3,000 and 6,000 tourists in town. The town's popularity stemmed from its pure mineral waters that bubbled up from the earth at 143 degrees.

Hot Springs was situated in the foothills of the Ozark Mountains, and the mountain trails proved challenging for the long runs on which Anson liked to lead his players. Afterward, they could relieve any aches and pains—or sweat off winter weight—by "boiling out" in one of the 17 bathhouses in town.

There were many complaints from the players, but Cap's team won another pennant in 1886.

Although he was obstinate and often difficult to get along with, he was noted for his sobriety in an era when many players drank excessively and behaved rowdily. During the 1886 season, he had the players take a no-drinking pledge in the owner's office.

The naming of James Hart to the presidency of the Chicago team in 1892 marked the beginning of the end of Anson's association with the club. Anson never got along with Hart, and their feud eventually led to Anson's being fired after the 1897 season. Known as the Colts then, the team briefly became known as the Orphans, because the players had lost their Pop.

Hart offered to hold a benefit game for Anson, but Anson indignantly turned down the offer. Instead, he was hired by John Montgomery Ward to manage the Giants. However, that union lasted only 25 days.

After leaving the Giants, Anson opened a billiard saloon. He tried to organize a rival major league called the American Association in 1899, but it failed. He entered vaudeville, accompanied by his two daughters, and performed skits written by the renowned Ring Lardner. Later he served a term as city clerk in Chicago.

In 1920, at the age of 68, Anson campaigned for the job as the first commissioner of baseball, but he was ignored, and the position went to Judge Kenesaw Mountain Landis. When Anson died two years later, his funeral expenses were paid for by the National League.

Honus Wagner

Ranking: 7th
Hit Total: 3,420

Courtesy of Pittsburgh Pirates

It was early in the National League season, and Honus Wagner, a rookie with the Louisville Colonels, was batting against the Baltimore Orioles, a rowdy bunch with a reputation for hard-nosed baseball.

Wagner, a friendly, humble fellow, drilled a pitch into the left center field gap and started to circle the bases. As he rounded first base, Orioles first baseman Jack Doyle stuck out his hip and bumped the rookie, knocking him slightly off stride.

When he reached second base, shortstop Hughie Jennings forced him to go wide and upset his stride. At third base, John McGraw blocked him off the bag, then knocked the wind out of him by tagging him hard in the stomach.

What should have been an easy home run had been reduced to a triple, and Colonels manager Fred Clarke was livid.

"What the hell kind of ballplaying is that?" screamed Clarke when Wagner returned to the bench. "If you can't do any better than that, you won't be with us when we leave here tomorrow."

Wagner got the message. On his next at-bat, he hit a grounder to McGraw at third. McGraw's throw to first appeared to have Wagner beaten, but the rookie banged into Doyle at first and knocked him out of the play. McGraw's throw sailed deep into foul territory, and Wagner scored before the Orioles could retrieve the ball.

When he reached the dugout, Clarke was the first to greet him. "That's the way to play ball," Clarke said, patting Wagner on the back.

The rookie had made a lasting impression on one of baseball's best teams. In the years to come, he would grow into a legend.

JOHANNES Peter Wagner is regarded by many former players and officials as the greatest all-around player who ever lived. One of the five players selected as the first members of the Baseball Hall of Fame, Wagner won a record eight National League batting titles, hit over .300 for 17 consecutive seasons, and compiled a lifetime batting average of .329. Six times he led the league in slugging percentage and five times in RBI.

But he was far more than just a productive hitter. He also was one of the preeminent base stealers of all time (722 stolen bases), and he was regarded as the best fielder of his era with a howitzer-like arm that would leave teammates' hands swollen.

"So uniformly good was Wagner as a player," John McGraw, who became a legendary manager of the New York Giants, once wrote, "that it is almost impossible to determine whether his highest point of superiority was in his fielding, in his batting or in his base running."

Baseball historians claim that Wagner, known as "The Flying Dutchman," could have won the National League's Most Valuable Player Award six times between 1900 and 1910 if the prize had then been in existence.

Wagner certainly did not resemble a baseball player. He was a muscular 5-foot-11, 200 pounds with bowed legs and a barrel chest. He had long arms and huge hands that hung so low that Hall of Famer Lefty Gomez once quipped that Wagner could tie his shoes without bending over.

"He's a squat, 200-pound man whose legs take off at the ankles in an outward and upward direction and join his torso at the belt with some element of surprise," a sportswriter once wrote in describing Wagner's physique.

As a hitter, he had few equals. A right-handed batter, he stood deep in the batter's box, well off the plate, and had an unusually wide stance. He gripped the bat about three inches from the end with his hands spread about a palm's length apart. He had a short, compact stroke and was primarily a line-drive hitter who hit to all fields with equal ability.

He was a power hitter in the era of the dead ball, collecting 651 doubles, 232 triples and 101 home runs among his 3,430 hits.

Wagner was almost as famous a base runner as he was a hitter. He was certainly among the fastest big men of all time. He ran with reckless abandon, never hesitating to take the extra base or force an error by the opposition. He was a master of the hook slide, often eluding the most inevitable of tags.

"Now you'd see the big, clumsy guy and you wouldn't think he couldn't run a lick, but he would seem to stride twice as far as [Ty] Cobb and faster," recalled former teammate George Gibson.

The Flying Dutchman recorded 20 or more stolen bases for 18 consecutive seasons, with a single high of 61 in 1907. Five times he stole four bases in a game, and on two occasions, he swiped second, third, and home in succession. In all, he stole home 14 times during his career.

As a fielder, Wagner was unusually versatile. During his 21-year major league career, 18 of which were spent with the Pittsburgh Pirates, he played every position except catcher. "He was a great outfielder and the marvel of his day in the infield," said John McGraw.

Wagner is best known as a shortstop, yet that was the last position he came to play. It was not until 1901, his fifth year in the big leagues, that he became a shortstop, and he revolutionized the position. He was not graceful, but his range was extraordinary, and his long arms enabled him to field balls that other shortstops could not reach.

"He just ate up the ball with his big hands, like a scoop shovel," remembered longtime teammate Tommy Leach, "and when he threw it to first base you'd see pebbles and dirt and everything else flying over there along with the ball."

Wagner also had a remarkably strong throwing arm. "He threw harder than any man in the business," recalled Kitty Bransfield, who played first base for the Pirates for four years beginning in 1901. "When the ball strikes my mitt, it feels like a ton of lead."

In addition to his physical attributes, Wagner was usually a step ahead of his peers because of his uncanny instincts on the playing field. He was a student of the game, learning the habits and tendencies of opposing pitchers and batters. He was always alert and rarely committed a mental error. "I never saw him do the wrong thing," said McGraw.

Wagner's greatest gift to the game, however, may have been in his behavior off the field. In an era when many ballplayers were hard-drinking, carousing roughnecks, Wagner was a modest and unassuming gentleman. He cared little for money and lived frugally, even when he was making more money than anyone else in the game.

In an age when many ballplayers smoked, Wagner was a staunch opponent of smoking. When a tobacco company issued a small number of baseball cards as promotional giveaways back in 1910, Wagner made it remove his card from the series. Today an original Honus Wagner tobacco card can fetch $500,000 or more from baseball card collectors.

Wagner was a man of simple tastes, preferring the comfort of corduroys or jeans to a suit and tie and the taste of ham and eggs to frogs' legs

and caviar. He liked hunting and fishing instead of the lights of Broad-
way. He loved children and, like Babe Ruth years later, related to them on
their own terms.

As a veteran ballplayer and later as a coach, Wagner befriended the
rookies and was always willing to impart some of his knowledge of the
game. This was simply not done when Wagner was a rookie, and it was an
indication of his gentle and kind nature.

Born on February 24, 1874, in Mansfield, Pennsylvania, Wagner was
one of six children, five of them boys, of German immigrants. His father,
Peter, worked in a coal mine, and young Johannes, or Hans, as he was
known, left school at the age of 12 to work in the mine.

Despite long hours, Honus found time to play both basketball and
baseball and became quite good at both sports. Honus's brothers also were
good at sports, and the family formed a team called the Wagner Brothers
ball club.

"That's how I came to play pretty good in all positions," Honus once
observed. "Our family team, you had to know how to play everywhere, as
we were always shifting."

Hans played semipro baseball around his hometown of Mansfield
and Dennison, Ohio, from 1892 to 1894. His older brother, Al, had signed
a contract with Steubenville, Ohio, of the Interstate League, and it was Al
who convinced the Steubenville manager, George Moreland, that Hans
could help their team.

Moreland wired Hans an offer of $35 a month, and the youngster
couldn't wait to join the team. When Moreland came down for breakfast
the next morning, there was Hans waiting for him in the lobby with a
newspaper tucked under his arm. He hadn't even waited for a passenger
train but had hopped aboard a westward-bound freight at Mansfield.

Hans had no baseball shoes, though, and he played his first game for
Steubenville in his stocking feet. He showed he could hit, though, batting
.402 in 44 games. Later that season, he hit .365 in 20 games for Adrian of
the Michigan State League and .369 for Warren, Pennsylvania, of the
Iron-Oil League. For Wagner's three teams of 1895, he played infield and
outfield and even caught.

In 1896, an Eastern club owner named Ed Barrow was looking for
good players for his Paterson, New Jersey, team of the Atlantic League. He
knew of the players of the Western Pennsylvania-Eastern Ohio country
and offered a job to Al Wagner. Al, who was a locomotive engineer when
he wasn't playing ball, said to Barrow, "You don't want me, Ed; you want
my brother, John. He's a better player than I am." Al then told Barrow
how to get to Mansfield.

Arriving at Mansfield, Barrow asked some men loitering around the railroad station where he could find John Wagner. He was pointed in the right direction, and one of the men agreed to accompany him. They came across some boys throwing chunks of coal at a freight car, and the boys began running as Barrow and his guide approached. The boys thought the pair were railroad detectives. One of the boys was John Wagner, and when Barrow finally caught up with him, he signed him right there on the railroad tracks for $100 a month.

Hans Wagner was a star in the Eastern League right from the start. In his first season, Wagner, then 22, played mostly first base and hit .349. He was shifted to third the next year and batted .379. His hitting was beginning to attract the attention of National League teams.

In midsummer of 1897, Harry Pulliam, secretary of Barney Dreyfuss's Louisville club of the NL, offered Barrow $2,000 for Wagner. The owner of the Pittsburgh Pirates, Captain W.W. Kerr, knew all about Wagner and had a verbal agreement with Barrow that he would get first crack at the youngster when Barrow decided to put him on the market.

Kerr agreed to match Louisville's offer, but Dreyfuss authorized Pulliam to raise the ante by $100. Barrow advised Kerr of the new Louisville offer, but his telegram was ignored so Wagner was sold to Louisville for $2,100.

Wagner began his career in Louisville playing for a fiery young outfield-playing manager, Fred Clarke, who was only a year and a half older than Honus. Wagner hit .344 in 61 games for the Colonels in the latter part of the season, then hit .305 and .359 for the full seasons of 1898 and 1899.

After the 1899 season, the National League, which had operated for eight years as a 12-team league, voted to streamline back to eight teams. As a result Louisville, Cleveland, Baltimore, and Washington were dropped.

However, Barney Dreyfuss, president of the Colonels, liked baseball and decided to stay in the game. He purchased a half interest in the Pirates, was elected president of the team, and merged the better players from the 1899 Louisville and Pittsburgh teams. Thus Wagner became a member of the Pirates.

The strengthened team clicked immediately. Wagner, playing solely in the outfield, batted .381 to win his first NL batting title, and the Pirates, seventh in 1899, finished second in 1900. They went on to win the next three pennants, with Honus capturing his second batting title in 1903 with a .355 average.

The 1903 season ended on a sour note for Wagner, however. It was the year of the first modern World Series, and the Pirates met the American League champion Boston Red Sox in a best-of-nine series. Pittsburgh jumped out to a three-games-to-one lead but lost the last three games. Wagner was one of the major disappointments for Pittsburgh. He couldn't hit the Boston pitching stars Bill Dineen and Cy Young and batted just .214 in the eight games.

Wagner recovered from his ignominious performance in the 1903 World Series to win the batting title in five of the next six seasons. He repeatedly refused large monetary offers to jump to the American League. But after winning his fifth batting title in 1907, he insisted the Pirates pay him $10,000 a year, which was then the largest salary paid a major league player. He threatened to quit baseball and enter the garage business unless he got it. He held out during the 1908 training season and the first four days of the regular season before Dreyfuss gave in.

Despite Wagner's stellar play, the Pirates did not reach the World Series again until 1909, when they met the Detroit Tigers, led by Ty Cobb. It was a matchup of the two greatest players in the game, and Wagner got the better of the showdown.

The Pirates won the Series, which had been shortened in 1905 to a best-of-seven, four games to three, and Wagner hit .333 and stole six bases, while Cobb batted a meager .231 and stole just two bases.

Early in that series, Cobb reached first base for the first time and tried to intimidate Wagner. "Hey, Krauthead, I'm coming down on the next pitch," Cobb yelled in the direction of the Pirates' shortstop.

"I'll be waiting," Wagner answered.

Cobb took off on the first pitch and slid hard into second base. Wagner held his ground and tagged out Cobb with a forceful poke in the mouth that gave the Tigers' star a lacerated lip and loosened some of his teeth.

Wagner won his eighth and final batting title in 1911 at the age of 37. In 1912, he hit .324; he batted an even .300 in 1913. After that he had four more seasons in which his averages varied from .252 to .287. He finally retired after the 1917 season at the age of 43. In his final season, he played 74 games, mostly at second base, and also managed the team for five games in mid-season after Jimmy Callahan, Clarke's managerial successor, was fired.

Following his retirement, Wagner coached baseball for a while at Carnegie Tech and went into the sporting goods business with teammate Pie Traynor. He also held several political offices, was sergeant-at-arms in the Pennsylvania Legislature and served as fish commissioner.

On December 30, 1916, he married for the first time, and he became the father of two daughters. During the Depression of the 1930s, Wagners's sporting good store went bankrupt and the family suffered financially until Bill Benswanger, the son-in-law of Barney Dreyfuss, came to the rescue in 1933 by extending an invitation to Honus to rejoin the Pirates as a coach. He served in that capacity for 20 years and became a goodwill ambassador for the Pirates and baseball.

In the first vote for the Hall of Fame at Cooperstown, New York, in 1936, Wagner was one of the original five selected, along with Ty Cobb, Babe Ruth, Walter Johnson, and Christy Mathewson. In the spring of 1955, seven months before he died at the age of 81, a statue of Wagner was unveiled outside Schenley Park in Pittsburgh.

Carl Yastrzemski

Ranking: 8th
Hit Total: 3,419

AP/Wide World Photos

Carl Yastrzemski was three months into his rookie season with the Boston Red Sox and he was struggling. After a promising start, his batting average had fallen to .220, and he was beginning to wonder if he truly belonged in the major leagues.

Deep down inside, he knew what needed to be done.

"A man was fishing up in New Brunswick. I said, 'Can we get ahold of him? I need help. I don't think I can play in the big leagues,'" Yastrzemski recalled.

The Red Sox made the call to the "fisherman," and Ted Williams was soon on his way to Boston to help out the man who had replaced him in left field for the Red Sox.

"He worked with me for three days, helped me mentally, and gave me confidence that I could play in the big leagues," said Yastrzemski. "I hit .300 for the rest of the season."

One of the pieces of advice Williams gave Yastrzemski was this: "Don't ever let anyone monkey with your swing."

No one ever did, and the "scared rookie" went on to play 23 seasons with the Red Sox, compiling 3,419 hits. He won three American League batting titles, hit 452 home runs, and is one of only 11 players in history to win the Triple Crown of batting. He accomplished that feat in 1967 when he led the league in batting average (.326), home runs (44), and runs batted in (121).

Carl Michael Yastrzemski may have been the most popular player ever to wear a Red Sox uniform. His 23 years with Boston is the longest major league stint by a player with only one team. In a city that treats baseball like a religion, Yastrzemski—or just plain "Yaz," as he was known—approached sainthood.

He took over for a legend in left field and became one himself. Perhaps it was his work ethic that endeared him to Red Sox fans for so many years. Not as naturally gifted a hitter as his predecessor, Williams, Yastrzemski put in long hours to hone his skills, and the blue-collar workers who made Fenway Park their second home appreciated his effort.

"I never stay away from workouts. I work hard. I've tried to take care of my body. I'll never look back and say that I could have done more. I've paid the price in practice, but I know I get the most out of my ability," said Yastrzemski.

Joe Lahoud, a former teammate of Yastrzemski's, remembers Yaz taking hours of extra batting practice.

"Yaz did it all the time," said Lahoud. "We'd be on the road, and he'd call, 'C'mon, we're going out to the ballpark.' I'd say, 'Christ, it's only one o'clock. The game's at seven.' He lived, breathed, ate, slept baseball. If he went 0-for-4, he couldn't live with it. He could live with himself if he went 1-for-3. He was happy if he went 2-for-4. That's the way the man suffered."

The person who admired Yastrzemski most was Red Sox owner Tom Yawkey. Some felt their closeness undermined Boston managers.

"Yawkey loved his players," said Lahoud. "He loved Yastrzemski more than any of them. And he loved his players more than he loved his managers."

Red Sox fans are a demanding lot, though, and Yaz's career had all the ups and downs of a Boston Marathon. He had great seasons, to be sure, but many of those were often followed by poor ones that would leave even his staunchest rooters shaking their heads, perplexed by his inconsistency.

Still, few players responded to big-game pressure better than Yastrzemski. In 22 pennant-deciding and postseason games, Yaz batted .417 with six home runs and 25 RBI. During his career, Yaz received more intentional walks than anyone in the history of the American League.

"He was the type of player who would make your knees shake when he walked up to the plate, even in left field," said outfielder Lou Brock, a fellow member of the Hall of Fame. "You knew that with one swing of his bat, he was capable of turning the game around and he might hit the ball your way."

Only two pairs of players have succeeded one another at the same position on the same team and then followed each other into the Hall of Fame—center fielders Joe DiMaggio and Mickey Mantle of the New York Yankees and left fielders Williams and Yastrzemski.

Yet, it wasn't ever easy for Yastrzemski, who once admitted the game of baseball was never very much fun for him. His desire to succeed was often punishing, and because he did not have the natural batting skills of a DiMaggio, Mantle, or Williams, he had to work extra-hard to overcome his shortcomings.

Comparing Yastrzemski to Williams was unfair. Both were left-handed hitters, but that's the only thing they had in common. Yastrzemski was much smaller than Williams. While Williams was a dead pull hitter, many of Yastrzemski's drives went to straightaway center field. Yastrzemski was clearly a better fielder than Williams. Yaz had a much stronger arm and more speed.

Those who saw Yastrzemski play in his early minor league days must have wondered how he ever made the major leagues, much less the Hall of Fame. The son of a potato farmer from Long Island, Yastrzemski broke into professional baseball as a shortstop but was moved to second base in his first pro season. Despite leading the Carolina League in batting with a .377 average, he made 45 errors for Raleigh, North Carolina. That prompted a shift to the outfield the next season, as the Red Sox promoted him to Minneapolis of the Triple A American Association.

Yaz continued his fine hitting with the Millers, posting a .339 batting average while leading the league in hits (193). Williams was nearing the end of a magnificent career with the Red Sox, and the Boston front office felt Yaz was ready to succeed him. On opening day 1961, Yaz officially replaced Williams as the left fielder for the Red Sox.

With the aid of Williams's help that first season, Yastrzemski finished his rookie season with a .266 batting average. He raised it 30 points to .296 in his second campaign, and in 1963—his third season in the big leagues—he won the first of three batting titles with a .321 average.

Then began a stretch of peculiar up-and-down seasons for Yastrzemski. His average dropped to .289 the year after he won his first batting title, but he hit .312 the following season. He plummeted to .278 in 1966, only to rebound in 1967 by winning the Triple Crown, as the Red Sox won the American League pennant. That year he would hit a career-high 44 home runs, the first time in seven seasons that he hit more than 20.

Typically, neither the Red Sox nor Yastrzemski got off to a good start in 1967. The Red Sox, who had finished in ninth place the previous year, were only 11-14 and in a tie for eighth place on May 14, and Yaz was hitting just .260 with two home runs.

In June, manager Eddie Stanky of the Chicago White Sox publicly questioned Yastrzemski's intelligence on the ball field.

"Yastrzemski's an All-Star from the neck down," said Stanky.

Playing against the White Sox the next day, Yaz went 6-for-9 in a doubleheader. Yastrzemski homered in his last at-bat, and as he trotted around the bases, he tipped his cap to Stanky. Yastrzemski was on his way to one of the best all-around seasons in baseball history.

The pressure was demanding on both Yastrzemski and the Red Sox as the pennant race entered the final weekend of the season. The Red Sox were in a dogfight with the Minnesota Twins and Detroit Tigers in the pennant race, and the Twins' Harmon Killebrew was challenging Yastrzemski for the home run title.

Minnesota entered the final weekend one game ahead of Boston and Detroit. The Twins were in Boston for the last two games of the season while the Tigers had back-to-back doubleheaders left with the Angels. The Red Sox needed to win both games, with the Tigers doing no better than a split with the Angels.

In his effort to win the Triple Crown, Yastrzemski was in reasonably good shape for the batting and RBI titles, but he was tied with Killebrew at 43 homers apiece. With four games left to Yastrzemski's two, Killebrew had the edge.

Everything went well for the Red Sox on Saturday. Killebrew homered for Minnesota, but so did Yaz, who knocked in four runs, as the Red Sox came from behind to beat the Twins, 6-4. Meanwhile, the Tigers split with the Angels. The Twins and Red Sox were now tied for first place with Detroit one-half game behind.

It came down to the final day. The Twins went ahead early, 2-0, but the Red Sox loaded the bases in the fifth, and Yastrzemski stepped up to the plate. He lined a two-run single to center to tie the score. The Red Sox got three more runs in that inning and won the game, 5-2. Yaz went 4-for-4 and, although he didn't hit a home run, neither did Killebrew. Yastrzemski had won his Triple Crown with a .326 average, 121 RBI, and 44 homers.

"The moment the game was over, I sprinted for the dugout," Yastrzemski recalled. "The fans were pouring onto the field. If they'd caught me, they'd have torn my uniform into shreds for souvenirs. As it was, I got pawed all over."

The Tigers won the first game of the doubleheader Sunday to remain within a half-game of the Red Sox, but as all of Boston tuned in on radio, the Angels won the second game, 8-5. The Red Sox had won their first pennant since 1946, an "Impossible Dream" season that ended in reality.

Boston's opponent in the World Series was the St. Louis Cardinals, who had won the National League pennant by 10 1/2 games. The Cardinals were led by pitcher Bob Gibson, who had missed one-third of the season with a broken leg. Gibson, his leg completely recovered, was one of the most feared pitchers in the National League.

This was Yastrzemski's first test under postseason pressure, and he rose to the challenge. He homered twice in Game 2 in a 5-0 Boston victory, and he, Reggie Smith, and Rico Petrocelli homered in succession in the fourth inning of Game 6 to set a Series record and propel the Red Sox to an 8-4 victory that evened the Series at three games apiece.

It came down to one game.

The final game pitted Lonborg against Gibson, and it proved to be a mismatch in favor of the Cardinals. Gibson was masterful. He allowed only three hits, struck out 10, and hit a home run, as the Cardinals won, 7-2, to capture the World Series for the second time in four years. Yastrzemski hit .400 in the Series, but the Cardinals' Lou Brock was the batting star, hitting .414, with 12 hits, eight runs, and a Series-record seven stolen bases.

Yaz won another batting title in 1968, and in some ways it was his most remarkable. He batted only .301 but was the only hitter in the league to crack the .300 barrier. It was truly the year of the pitcher, as five AL starting pitchers posted earned run averages under 2.00. Detroit's Denny McLain won 31 games to become the first pitcher since Dizzy Dean in 1934 to crack that barrier.

Yastrzemski's batting average dropped 46 percentage points to .255 in 1969, yet he regained the home run stroke that had led the Red Sox to the 1967 pennant. Yaz hit 40 homers and drove in 111 runs to help the Red Sox finish third in the AL East, the first year of two-division play.

In 1970, he hit 40 homers again, knocked in 102 runs, batted .329, and led the league in slugging percentage (.592), runs scored (125), and on-base percentage. Although the Red Sox again finished third in the AL East, Yaz was fourth in the MVP voting.

Much of Yastrzemski's career, however, was a roller-coaster ride. Up one year, down the next. After his stellar 1970 campaign, he lost his hitting groove again and struggled through two straight seasons. He hit just .254 and .264 for the next two years and had a total of only 27 home runs.

Then he was back, hitting .296 in 1973 with 19 homers and 95 RBI and batting .301 with a league-leading 93 runs scored in 1974.

In 1975, Yastrzemski hit a three-run homer in the All-Star Game, but he slumped again to .269 with just 14 homers. Nonetheless, the Red Sox won the AL East title because of the stellar performances of rookies Fred Lynn and Jim Rice. Each hit better than .300, swatted more than 20 homers, and drove in more than 100 runs.

The Oakland A's, winners of the previous three World Series, won their fifth consecutive AL West title and were favored to beat the Red Sox in the best-of-five AL Championship Series. But once again, Yaz performed spectacularly under pressure, hitting .455 to help the Red Sox pull off a three-game sweep. In Game 3 he cracked two hits and made two defensive gems to lead the Red Sox into the World Series.

In one of the most dramatic World Series ever played, the Cincinnati Reds defeated the Red Sox in seven games despite a strong showing from Yastrzemski, who hit .310 with seven runs scored and four RBI.

Yaz, who hadn't hit 20 homers in a season in five years, hit 21 in 1976 and also drove in 100 runs (102) for the first time since 1970. The following year he, Rice, and Butch Hobson each drove in at least 100 runs, but Boston finished in a tie for second place, three games behind the New York Yankees.

One of Yastrzemski's biggest disappointments came during the 1978 season. The Red Sox and Yankees finished in a first-place tie in the AL East, setting up a one-game playoff. Boston had a 2-0 lead in the seventh inning, but Bucky Dent's three-run homer put New York on top. The Yankees scored twice more in the eighth and were ahead, 5-2, when the Red Sox mounted a comeback in the ninth.

They scored twice and had the winning run on base when Yastrzemski strode to the plate with two out. Red Sox fans were standing and cheering, anticipating yet another game-winning performance from their beloved Yaz.

Rich "Goose" Gossage, one of the top relievers in baseball, was pitching for the Yankees, and Yastrzemski knew he would get nothing but screaming fastballs.

"The pitch came in, on the inside, just at the knees," Yaz remembered. "My pitch. I swung, but just as I got the bat out, the ball exploded on me, coming in quicker than I had thought. I tried to turn on it, but I got underneath the ball."

The ball went straight up in the air to the left side of the infield, where third baseman Graig Nettles caught it. The game was over and so was Boston's season.

Yastrzemski played five more seasons after that, but the Red Sox never got close to the postseason again. Yastrzemski retired after the 1983 season with 3,419 hits, including 452 home runs. His career batting average was .285, and he hit better than .300 six times. His uniform No. 8 was retired by Boston.

"I was lucky enough to have the talent to play baseball," said Yastrzemski. "That's how I treated my career. I didn't think I was anybody special, anybody different."

Yaz belongs to an elite club of players who have 3,000 hits, including 400 home runs. Only Hank Aaron, Willie Mays, Eddie Murray, Stan Musial, and Dave Winfield have equaled that achievement.

"I'm very pleased and very proud of my accomplishments, but I'm most proud of that," Yaz commented. "Not [Ted] Williams, not [Lou] Gehrig, not [Joe] DiMaggio did that. They were Cadillacs and I'm a Chevrolet."

But one that ran beautifully on all cylinders.

Yaz recorded hit No. 3,000 on September 12, 1979, off New York's Jim Beattie. He confessed to feeling immense strain once he got closer to 3,000.

"The 3,000-hitting thing was the first time I let individual pressure get to me. I was uptight about it. When I saw the hit going through, I had a sigh of relief more than anything."

Paul Molitor

Ranking: 9th
Hit Total: 3,319

AP/Wide World Photos

Things were not going well for Cecil Cooper, the slugging first baseman of the Milwaukee Brewers. They hadn't been for some time. He had not had a hit, or even a run batted in, in quite a spell. Moreover, his confidence level was at rock bottom.

As he strode to the plate with one out in the ninth inning on this summer day in 1980, he had already gone 0-for-5. The Brewers were comfortably ahead in the game, and their fine young infielder, Paul Molitor, was on third base.

Cooper swung and hit a slow roller toward the second baseman.

"I thought, 'Oh, no, nothing for six on the night.' So I go dragging my butt down the first-base line all ticked off at myself, and all of a sudden I see the first baseman throwing home. I turn around and there's Molitor sliding in head first. I'm standing there feeling sorry for myself, and here's this guy stealing me an RBI."

As soon as he was done telling the story, Cooper reached into his locker and pulled out a pale blue T-shirt. On the front of the shirt was a picture of a spark plug and the words: "Molitor The Igniter."

"I usually wear it," said Cooper. "The man is my hero."

Paul Molitor was only 23 at the time and in only his third big-league season. Yet he had already begun carving a reputation for scrappy play that would be his trademark throughout his 21-year career.

Paul Leo Molitor's trademark was a dirty uniform. He didn't invent the headfirst slide, but he was among its staunchest proponents. He was a blue-collar-type player who, for most of his major league career, played in the blue-collar city of Milwaukee, Wisconsin, which fully appreciated the hustle and determination Molitor brought to the baseball field every day.

He was indeed a spark plug, constantly setting the table for the big sluggers of the Brewers and later the Toronto Blue Jays and Minnesota Twins. Unlike engine spark plugs, however, Molitor improved with age. For the first 13 years of his career, his hell-bent-for-leather approach landed him repeatedly on the disabled list. But he enjoyed some of the best years of his career after the age of 35, including three 200-hit seasons, his only two 100-RBI campaigns, and a World Series MVP award.

For most of his career, Molitor was a teammate of Hall-of-Famer Robin Yount, forming one of baseball's most potent batting combinations. Both players made baseball's 3,000 hit club, although Molitor's milestone hit came as a member of the Twins.

Molitor spent the first 15 years of his career (1978-92) with the Brewers, then played for Toronto from 1993 to 1995 and for Minnesota from 1996 to 1998. He played on his only World Series championship team with the Blue Jays in 1993.

Over his 21-year career, Molitor compiled a lifetime batting average of .306. He had 200 or more hits in a season four times, scored 100 or more runs five times, and hit .300 or better 12 times. Although not known for his power, he collected 605 doubles and hit 234 career homers, reaching double figures in 13 seasons.

His ability to get on base measured his true value, however. He had a lifetime on-base percentage of .369, including four seasons of .400 or higher. In addition, he stole 504 bases in his career, including 40 or more bases in a season four times.

What might he have achieved had not injuries hampered his career? Molitor was on the disabled list 12 times from 1980 to 1990. He missed large portions of the 1980, 1981, 1984, 1986, 1987, and 1990 seasons with a variety of ailments, most of them caused by his hard-nosed style of play. He ran the bases with reckless abandon and was never timid about barreling into an opposing infielder if it meant he could prevent a double play. But no matter how many times he ended up on the disabled list, he always worked himself back and was renowned throughout the American League for his work ethic and professionalism.

Molitor was also a versatile fielder, playing second base, third base, outfield, and first base at various times for the Brewers and doing well at all of them. From 1990 until the end of his career in 1998, he was used primarily as a designated hitter, a change that greatly reduced his injuries. Molitor brought a new dimension to the designated hitter's role. Whereas most teams used long-ball hitters in that position, Molitor proved a speedy, contact hitter could be just as productive.

Born on August 22, 1956, in St. Paul, Minnesota, Molitor was one of eight children from a family that was right out of a Norman Rockwell painting. He was a gifted athlete right from the start, and he grew up playing against older players because he was too good for his own age group.

When he was seven, a former professional baseball writer told Molitor that he was a professional baseball prospect, but as he grew older, there were two things that appeared to be major roadblocks to his future in sports—lack of size and a penchant for injury.

"I was 5-foot-4 my sophomore year in high school, and I was supposed to be too small to make it, but by the time I was a senior, I was 5-foot-10," said Molitor, who eventually grew to be a 6-foot, 180-pound athlete.

The other major question was whether he would remain in one piece. He suffered nine broken bones from various accidents and injuries before reaching the major leagues.

Molitor attended Cretin High School in St. Paul and was captain of the baseball, basketball, and soccer teams. He was mostly a pitcher in baseball and was drafted by the St. Louis Cardinals in the 25th round in 1974. He was all ready to sign with the Cardinals when Dick Seibert, the head baseball coach at the University of Minnesota, called and offered him a scholarship.

Molitor took the scholarship, but his pitching career ended in fall practice when his arm couldn't take pitching and playing shortstop. Seibert, an ex-major leaguer, liked Molitor's hustle and intelligence, and he schooled the youngster hard in fundamentals.

"I believe playing for Seibert helped me make it to the majors more quickly," Molitor said. "Playing in Minnesota, in the winter most of the workouts are indoors. You're limited to not doing anything but fundamentals.

"When I came out of college, I was as fundamentally strong as most major leaguers. I knew how to bunt, I knew how to execute on defense, I knew how to run the bases."

Molitor made college All-America at shortstop in his sophomore year. He tailed off a bit in his junior season, but the Brewers made him the third player selected in the 1977 June draft, and he signed with them for $100,000.

The Brewers sent him to Burlington, and he tore apart the Midwest League. In 64 games, Molitor hit .346 and knocked in 50 runs.

"Denis Menke was the manager, and he was a big help to me," said Molitor. "He changed my hitting style. Denis made me more of a stand-up hitter. Less power, but with more consistent contact."

Part of Molitor's contract included a major league salary for 1978, and the Brewers' front office told him he would get a chance to make the major league team as a second baseman. But before spring training began, the Brewers had a new general manager and a new field manager, George Bamberger.

"I thought we had a kid that someday was going to be a hell of a ballplayer. But there was no doubt in my mind that he'd be down in the minor leagues somewhere," said Bamberger.

Two weeks before the season opened, Molitor was informed that he would begin the season in Triple A. The next day he signed his option papers and went back to the hotel to pack. He then checked out of the hotel and waited for roommate Jim Gantner to pick him up and take him to the minor league complex.

When Gantner arrived, he told Molitor to stick around. A few minutes later, Milwaukee vice president Tom Ferguson arrived and told him the same thing. Robin Yount, the team's shortstop, was contemplating retiring and taking up professional golf. The Brewers were in need of a shortstop, and Molitor was going to be given an opportunity to win the job.

Molitor won the job by hitting .400 the rest of the spring. When Yount finally did return, the Brewers were so impressed with Molitor that they moved him to second base. He played in 125 games his rookie year and batted .273.

He became a star the following season by hitting .322 and collecting 188 hits in 140 games. Then the injuries started. In 1980, Molitor suffered torn muscles in his rib cage and played only 111 games. A year later he tore the ligaments in his ankle when he tried to beat out a ground ball to shortstop and missed nearly 100 games.

It was during the injury-plagued 1981 season that Molitor took a dangerous road that nearly forced him to lose his way. Saddled with too much idle time and money, he began experimenting with illegal drugs. First, it was marijuana, then cocaine. Realizing he was jeopardizing not only his career but his life, he managed to steady himself and quit cold turkey.

"I was young and I made some mistakes, which I regret," he said. "Part of it was peer pressure. I was young and single and hung around with some wrong people. I was able to get out before I got into serious trouble."

In 1982, he managed to get through an injury-free season and helped the Brewers to the American League pennant. He hit .302 and scored a league-leading 136 runs. In the World Series against the St. Louis Cardinals, he became the first player ever to get five hits in a single Series game. But the Brewers ended up blowing a three-games-to-one lead and lost the Series in seven games.

His injury-plagued career continued in 1983 and 1984. In 1983, he suffered a fractured bone in his right wrist, and in 1984, he underwent an operation in which a tendon from his left wrist was used to replace the ligament in his right elbow. He played only 13 games in 1984.

While such surgery usually takes players half a year to come back, Molitor got into 140 games in 1985 and hit .297 while scoring 93 runs. But injuries caught up with him again in 1986 and 1987, limiting him to fewer than 120 games in each of those seasons. In 1987, Molitor was on the disabled list on three separate occasions because of a hamstring injury. The Brewers had a 75-42 record with him in the lineup. Without him, they were 16-29.

Even with the injuries in 1987, Molitor managed to make headlines with a 39-game hitting streak from July 16 through August 25. It was the longest streak in the American League since Joe DiMaggio's record 56-game streak in 1941.

Unlike most players, Molitor became a better hitter as he got older. From his rookie year of 1978 through 1986, Molitor hit over .300 only three times. But from 1987—when he turned 31—until his retirement after the 1998 campaign, he hit over .300 nine times, including a career high of .353 in 1987.

Part of the reason for that may have been his switch to designated hitter at the beginning of the 1991 season. The move was made to help Molitor avoid injury, and it certainly helped. From 1991 through 1996, he played in 158 or more games four times.

"The logic of the move was that DHing would reduce my chance of injury, and it proved correct," said Molitor. "That doesn't mean I like it. You're at bat maybe 10 minutes out of a three-hour game, and that means you have an awful lot of time on your hands."

Molitor filled the DH position for the Brewers for two seasons. In 1991, his first year as the DH, he enjoyed one of the best years of his career by batting .325 with 216 hits and 133 runs scored. He would certainly have been a candidate for MVP had the Brewers not been also-rans in the AL East.

He followed by hitting .320 with 195 hits in 1992, and it proved to be his last season with the Brewers. Although he was still a productive hitter, the Brewers asked him to take a pay cut for the 1993 season. Molitor was hurt by the offer and decided to become a free agent.

Eager to play again for a pennant contender, he signed with the defending World Series-champion Toronto Blue Jays. The Blue Jays had just lost their designated hitter, Dave Winfield, to retirement, and Molitor was the perfect fit.

Playing in 160 games for the Blue Jays, Molitor hit .322 with 211 hits and established a career high in homers (22) and knocked in 111 runs. The Blue Jays beat the Chicago White Sox in six games to repeat as AL champions, then met the Philadelphia Phillies, who upset the Atlanta Braves in the NL Championship Series, in the World Series.

Back in the World Series for the first time in 11 years, Molitor put on a show. At the age of 37, he played like a man 10 years younger. Playing first and third base as well as DH, he went 12-for-24 with two doubles, two triples, two home runs, and eight RBI. He also scored 10 runs, as the Blue Jays beat the Phillies in six games.

In the decisive sixth game, Molitor was the catalyst. He tripled home a run in the first inning, belted a solo homer in the fourth, and singled in the ninth ahead of Joe Carter's Series-winning home run. Not surprisingly, Molitor was named the Series MVP.

"Molly starts the party here," said Toronto slugger Joe Carter. "You've got a guy 37 years old that's playing like he's 24, 25. He's enthused about playing hard. People really saw what type of Hall of Fame player that guy can be. He's one of the best."

Molitor played one more season with the Blue Jays, then returned to his hometown to play for the Minnesota Twins. In 1996, he hit .341, while leading the league with a career-best 225 hits . . . at the age of 39. Molitor hit .305 in 1997, then .281 in 1998, his final season.

He collected his 3,000th hit in Kansas City off Royals rookie Jose Rosado on September 16, 1996. Fittingly, he slid into second with a double —headfirst, of course.

Molitor, who went into broadcasting after his retirement, will be eligible for election to the Hall of Fame in 2002. If the Hall of Fame ever asks for his uniform to display, it will undoubtedly be a dirty one.

Eddie Collins

Ranking: 10th
Hit Total: 3,315

AP/Wide World Photos

The fix was in the works for the 1919 World Series. The gamblers had successfully lured Chicago White Sox first baseman Chick Gandil as the contact man. It was his job to line up more players to go along with the scheme. The man the gamblers wanted on board the most was Chicago second baseman Eddie Collins. He was the White Sox captain and important in the conspirators' plans. They wondered if the plan would succeed without him.

Collins was 28 years old at the time and already on his way to a Hall of Fame career. His ability at the plate, speed on the bases, and sure-handedness in the field made him second only to Detroit's Ty Cobb among the league's top players.

But Gandil knew better than to even try to approach Collins.

"That's one guy we can't get," Gandil told the gamblers' agent. "And if he ever gets wise, we are sunk. He'll tell the world."

Such was the character of Eddie Collins. His reputation was so intimidating, Gandil would not even entertain the thought of approaching him.

As it turned out, the gamblers didn't need Collins. They made the fix stand up without him. And, ironically, Collins, off his play, was more suspect than some of his teammates who later admitted they accepted bribes to fix the Series in favor of the Cincinnati Reds.

A .319 hitter during the season, Collins hit just .226 in the Series, while Joe Jackson, one of those found guilty in the scandal, hit .375 and fielded 17 chances flawlessly in the outfield. It was later revealed that Jackson changed his mind about going along with the fix, but his refusal to report the incident climaxed in his being banned from baseball for life by Judge Kenesaw Mountain Landis, baseball's newly installed commissioner, with the rest of the infamous eight.

Others banned for life by Landis for their involvement were Gandil, short-stop Swede Risberg, third baseman Buck Weaver, infielder Fred McMullin, outfielder Happy Felsch, and pitchers Eddie Cicotte and Claude "Lefty" Williams.

It was Eddie Collins, however, who emerged through all the ugliness of the "Black Sox" scandal with his integrity completely intact and as a role model for the young people of the era.

Edward Trowbridge Collins played 25 seasons in the major leagues and ranks among the greatest players in the game's history. He collected 3,313 hits, batted over .300 in 19 seasons and compiled a .333 career batting average. He also led American League second basemen in fielding nine times. He posted a .328 batting average over six World Series and was named the American League's Most Valuable Player in 1914.

Yet, despite the fancy numbers, Collins was best known for his ability to outthink the opposition. He was different from most of his contemporaries in that he was a college graduate, receiving a diploma from Columbia University in 1907.

"He brought brains into baseball," said a former Red Sox scout Andy Coakley.

Collins's most famous moment was a direct result of his outthinking the opposition. It came in Game 6 of the 1917 World Series against the Giants at New York's Polo Grounds. Collins was at third and Joe Jackson at first for the White Sox, when Happy Felsch hit a high hopper back to Giants pitcher Rube Benton. Collins, in order to draw Benton's attention so that he would not wheel around and start a double play, faked a break for the plate, and Benton threw to catcher Bill Rariden.

Giants third baseman Heine Zimmerman cut behind Collins, and Rariden ran toward third with his arm cocked. Collins, hoping to stay in a rundown long enough for Jackson to get to third and Felsch to second, noticed out of the corner of his eye that neither Benton nor first baseman Walter Holke was backing up Rariden.

When Rariden threw the ball to Zimmerman, who had closed in behind Collins, Eddie quickly reversed his stride and broke for the plate, which was uncovered. Zimmerman then was left with the nearly impossible task of trying to run Collins down. As it turned out, he ended up chasing Collins across the plate with a run that proved pivotal in a Series-clinching 4-2 victory for the White Sox.

Speed was a large part of Collins's game. He twice stole six bases in a game and stole over 60 bases in a season three times, including a career-high 81 in 1910. He also stole 14 bases in World Series competition, a record he shares with fellow Hall of Famer Lou Brock of the St. Louis Cardinals.

Oddly, as a youngster growing up in Tarrytown, New York, it was football—not baseball—that interested Collins. In 1903, he enrolled as a 140-pound varsity quarterback at Columbia and played three seasons for the Lions. He was named team captain following his junior season, but the summer before his final year, he played semipro baseball in order to make some extra money.

A Philadelphia Athletics scout saw him play and recommended him to Athletics owner and manager Connie Mack. When Mack offered him a contract, Collins couldn't resist, even though he had another year of college remaining.

When Collins walked into Mack's office at the Philadelphia ballpark, the Athletics' manager was talking to a former ballplayer, Tim Murnane, who became a Boston sportswriter. Mack knew how much Collins loved football and wanted to protect his remaining year of college eligibility, so he quickly cornered the youngster.

"Hello, Sullivan," Mack said to the perplexed rookie while pushing him out the door. "Glad to see you."

Mack thought that Murnane, a writer from an Ivy League city, might have seen Collins play against Harvard. He advised Collins to stay out of uniform until the Red Sox left town.

So Collins remained Sullivan until he rejoined the Athletics a year later. Then, with Philadelphia teammates stubbornly calling him "Sully," a St. Louis newspaper commented, "The A's have a new rookie infielder listed under the name of Collins. Actually Collins is Sullivan. He played briefly with them last September."

Collins made his major league debut at shortstop against the White Sox in September of 1906. In his first time at bat, as a pinch hitter, he singled off Big Ed Walsh, who would go on to a Hall of Fame career.

It turned out that Collins lost his college football eligibility anyway, not because of the Sullivan caper, but because the school found out about his accepting money for playing semipro baseball under his own name in New England.

Unable to play for Columbia in 1906, he became coach.

"I believe it was the first time in any school that an undergraduate was paid to coach," Collins recalled years later.

A hard worker and a strong believer in off-season conditioning, Collins was known for conscientious determination to eliminate faults through constant practice.

"I used to take a buggy whip and switch him across the shins when he didn't stand in perfect balance while drilling on bunts," Coakley recalled. "He was a perfectionist. He wanted every move to be correct."

Nicknamed "Cocky" by his teammates for his self-assuredness, Collins hardly looked like a man to be feared at the plate. He stood 5-9 and weighed only 160 pounds for most of his career. He was a left-handed batter who choked up on the bat and sprayed the ball to all fields. He also was an expert drag bunter.

In the field, he appeared nonchalant and, at times, seemed to loaf after balls. Yet he always got in front of balls and played the hitters wisely.

"Eddie Collins was the greatest infielder I ever saw," said Frankie Frisch, a fellow member of the Hall of Fame and himself a standout second baseman. "He could do everything."

Collins was a reserve infielder and outfielder for the A's for most of his first three big-league seasons, but in 1909, he became the club's regular second baseman. Teaming with first baseman Stuffy McInnis, shortstop Jack Barry, and third baseman Frank "Home Run" Baker, Collins became the keystone of baseball's so-called $100,000 infield that led the Athletics to four pennants and three world championships between 1910 and 1914.

In his first year as the club's regular second baseman, Collins hit .346 and stole 67 bases. When the A's won the AL pennant in 1910, Eddie hit .429 and stole four bases in the World Series, as the A's beat the Chicago Cubs in five games.

The Athletics won the pennant again in 1911 and beat the New York Giants in six games in the World Series. It was in this Series that Baker earned the nickname "Home Run" by winning Games 2 and 3 with homers.

The A's did not win the pennant in 1912, but they were back in the Series again in 1913. This time Collins was one of the stars, batting .421 with three stolen bases in a five-game victory over the Giants.

Next to the Black Sox scandal, the biggest disappointment of Collins's career came in the 1914 World Series against the Boston Braves. The Athletics were heavily favored to win the Series against a Braves team that had come from last place in July to record a "miracle" finish.

But the Braves stunned the Athletics and won the Series in four straight games. George Stallings, manager of the Braves, had his team fired up from the very first game, and they verbally abused the A's from the start. Collins was the No. 1 target for the abuse because he was the A's best player, and the taunts succeeded in stopping him cold at the plate. After hitting .344 during the regular season, Collins hit just .214 and knocked in only one run in the Series.

After that Series, Mack, hurting for money, broke up the A's dynasty. Collins was sold to the White Sox for $50,000, which was a large sum of money in those days.

Collins was shocked at the deal and did not want to go to Chicago. He asked permission to make a deal with Joe Lannin, owner of the Red Sox, to stay in the East, but his plea was refused.

The White Sox faced tough competition from the new Federal League, with ex-Cubs' star Joe Tinker managing the Feds; and both White Sox owner Charles Comiskey and Ban Johnson, founder and president of the AL, wanted a strong team in Chicago.

Comiskey was regarded as a cheapskate by the Chicago players for his penny-pinching salaries, but Collins, coming off an MVP season, negotiated a contract that paid him twice that of the other members of the White Sox. Some of his new teammates resented him for his salary and his ways. He was college educated, well mannered, and at times aloof. While Collins became friends with catcher Ray Schalk, neither shortstop Swede Risberg nor first baseman Chick Gandil spoke to him.

Still, Collins continued to be one of the top players in the league. Two years after joining the White Sox, he led them to the World Series championship over the Giants, which he culminated with his mad dash for home in the decisive sixth game.

Collins had trouble getting untracked in 1918. Bothered by the outbreak of World War I, he batted only .276 in 97 games before enlisting in the Marine Corps in August. Before he could get overseas, the war ended and Collins returned to baseball for the 1919 season, which would prove to be the most heartbreaking of his career.

Yet Collins admitted shortly before his death in 1951 that he regarded the 1917 and 1919 White Sox teams as the greatest he ever saw because they were able to win despite widening dissension on the team.

"That was the amazing thing about that team," said Collins. "It was torn by discord and hatred during much of the 1919 season. From the very moment I arrived at training camp from service, I could see that something was amiss.

"We may have had our troubles in other years, but in 1919 we were a club that pulled apart rather than together. There were frequent arguments and open hostility.

"All the things you think—and are taught to believe—are vital to the success of any athletic organization were missing from it, and yet it was the greatest collection of players ever assembled, I would say."

For much of his life, Collins refused to talk about the Black Sox scandal. Yet in his later years, he admitted that the honest players on the team never suspected the conspirators.

"No one realizes how subtly conceived and executed the whole thing was," said Collins. "Sure, I heard the fix was on, but I looked on it as just idle gossip and completely preposterous. I hadn't been close to some of the fellows, but, still, they were my teammates. Why shouldn't I defend them?"

Following the Black Sox scandal of 1919, Comiskey became even more dependent on Collins for leadership. In 1925, Collins was made player/manager of the team, and he guided the team to successive fifth-place finishes while hitting .346 and .344, respectively. After the White Sox released him following the 1926 season, Eddie returned to Philadelphia as a player/coach under Mack.

Connie Mack had rebuilt the A's into a powerhouse, and the 1928 team included six players—Collins, Ty Cobb, Tris Speaker, Mickey Cochrane, Jimmie Foxx, and Lefty Grove—who would make the Hall of Fame. Cobb, Speaker, and Collins, however, were in the waning years of their careers.

The A's won three pennants and two World Series from 1929 to 1931, but Collins made his last appearance as a player in 1930, getting one hit in two at-bats. In 1929, he was offered the job of managing the New York Yankees following the death of Miller Huggins, but he turned it down on advice from Connie Mack.

Collins also had opportunities to manage the St. Louis Browns and the Washington Senators, but each time, he said no. Instead, he remained as a coach with the A's, imparting his vast knowledge of the game to a group of newcomers who restored the team to prominence.

Collins was still a coach with the Athletics in 1933 when he was approached by Tom Yawkey, the young owner of the Boston Red Sox. Yawkey had been a great admirer of Collins as a ballplayer and offered him the job as vice president and general manager of the Red Sox.

While Eddie was hesitating, Connie Mack made up his mind for him.

"If you don't take this job, Eddie," Mack said, "I shall have to fire you."

As the Red Sox's GM, Collins helped build the club from a ragtag outfit into a pennant contender. He engineered the deals that helped the Red Sox obtain Jimmie Foxx and Lefty Grove from Philadelphia, and he helped build a farm system.

At Yawkey's insistence, Collins took a scouting trip to the west coast to look at a shortstop prospect named Eddie Mayo. Collins was not that impressed with Mayo, but he liked the look of a second baseman and was impressed with the swing of a lanky outfielder. That's how Bobby Doerr and Ted Williams became members of the Red Sox.

Collins served as head of Boston's baseball operations from 1932 until his death in 1951. Yet he was not always given a free hand. The Red Sox were the last team to integrate their team following the breaking of the color barrier in 1947. One of the players Collins was forced to turn away after a Fenway Park tryout in the mid-1940s was Jackie Robinson.

Willie Mays

Ranking: 11th
Hit Total: 3,283

AP/Wide World Photos

Billy Cox stood at third base with the tie-breaking run in the eighth inning as Carl Furillo stepped to the plate for the Brooklyn Dodgers on August 15, 1951, against the club's hated rival, the New York Giants. Furillo was as dangerous a clutch hitter as there was in the major leagues, and this time he hit a slicing line drive to right-center that seemed certain to get the run home.

As soon as the ball was hit, Cox retreated to the base and tagged up, waiting for the ball to fall in safely before breaking for the plate, even though that fact was practically guaranteed.

Out in center field, the Giants' 20-year-old Willie Mays, only in the major leagues a few short months, broke at the crack of the bat. He appeared to have little chance of catching the ball as it was fading away from him toward right field. But at the last second, Mays made a lunge at the ball and caught it at his shoe tops. Then, as Cox broke for home, Mays leaped in the air, spun his body counterclockwise in one fluid motion and unleashed a powerful, 300-foot perfect strike to catcher Wes Westrum that nailed the stunned Cox by 10 feet.

This play epitomized the genius that was Willie Mays as a baseball player. If he had made the play in an orthodox manner, he would have stopped short after making the catch, then turned and thrown the ball home. But the throw would have been too late to get Cox. Instead, his instincts told him to make the play in an unorthodox fashion if he was to get Cox at the plate.

Later, after the Giants had won the game, losing manager Charley Dressen, never one to be at a loss for words, could only say, "I'd like to see him do that again."

Mays never did do that exact same play again. But he made hundreds of others nearly as spectacular and just as unexpected. Branch Rickey, when he *was running the Pittsburgh Pirates, remembered a play in Pittsburgh's Forbes Field, when Mays caught up with a 400-foot hooking drive off the bat of Rocky Bridges and, with his back to the infield and the ball trailing down and to the right, reached out and caught it bare-handed at knee level.*

Then there was "The Catch" in the first game of the 1954 World Series at New York's Polo Grounds off Cleveland's Vic Wertz, which is televised every October on the Series' highlight film. That's the play where Mays made an over-the-shoulder grab of what appeared to be a sure triple, then whirled around and made a bullet throw to second base to hold the runners while falling to the ground. The catch saved the game for the Giants, who then went on to complete a four-game sweep.

Mays could do everything on a baseball field, and better than anyone else. Nicknamed the "Say Hey Kid" because of his infectious, high-pitched greeting, Mays played baseball with an élan and a boyish enthusiasm seldom seen even on the sandlots. There were the basket catches, the howitzer-like throws, the clutch home runs, the rally-starting stolen bases, the exciting first-to-third dashes. What also set him apart was that he demonstrated these skills with panache and a flair for the dramatic.

"I always try to do something different," Mays said once. "I don't try to do what the other fellow does. People come to ball games to see fellows do something different."

Willie Howard Mays was different all right. "I've seen most of the great players, and there was not a one of them who could match Willie for all-round performance," said Giants scout Tom Sheehan. "Take them all, I don't care—Speaker, Cobb, Gehrig, Ruth, Traynor, Meusel. Then take DiMag, Williams, Musial, Mantle—or whoever else you can name. Sure they are good. Some of them are great. Some of them can hit and field.

Some of them can run and throw. But Willie can do just about what they can in their special departments, and what's more, he's the only one of them who can do everything a ballplayer has to do."

Statistics don't do Willie Mays justice any more than record sales did justice to Frank Sinatra's contribution to music. Yet Willie's statistics are staggering. During a 22-year career, 21 of which were spent with the Giants, he had 3,283 career hits, including 660 home runs, for a .302 lifetime batting average. He also led the National League in batting average once, in home runs four times, in slugging average five times, and in stolen bases four times. He knocked in 1,903 runs, including eight seasons in a row of more than 100, and he won 12 Gold Gloves for fielding excellence.

He was the first player to amass 300 homers and 300 steals, and he is one of only three players—Hank Aaron and Eddie Murray are the others—to collect 3,000 hits and 500 home runs.

Born on May 6, 1931, in Westfield, Alabama, a steel-mill town near the outskirts of Birmingham. Willie was practically raised on a baseball field. His father, Willie Sr., worked in the tool room of a steel mill and also was an outfielder and leadoff hitter for the famed Birmingham Black Barons of the Negro National League. Nicknamed "Kitty Kat" because of his fast hands, Willie Sr. would take his son to the ball field almost daily from the time he was three.

"When Willie was 14 months old, I gave him a rubber ball," said the elder Mays. "I used to come home from the steel mill, and every afternoon I'd roll that rubber ball across the floor to Willie—oh, 30 or 40 times—until I'd get tired. Willie never got tired. As soon as I stopped rolling the ball, he'd cry."

By the time Willie reached three, the elder Mays would engage his son in a game of catch on the ball field across the street from where they lived.

"By the time he was six, I'd come home from work and catch him across the street on the diamond all alone, playing by himself," his father said. "He'd throw the ball up and hit it with the bat and then run and tag all the bases—first, second, and third—and then when he got home, he'd slide. He learned that from watching me. I showed him how to slide."

All was not well in the Mays household, however. Before Willie reached school age, his parents divorced and Willie went to live with an aunt, Sarah Mays, in Fairfield, Alabama, another small industrial town adjacent to Birmingham. His father lived nearby.

Willie's father played in the local Industrial League, and Willie would always accompany him to the games. By the time Willie was 10, he was playing with 15-year-olds. When he was 14, Willie was excelling as a pitcher and earning some money with a semipro steel-mill team. He was also attending Fairfield Industrial High School and taking a trade course in pressing and cleaning.

Willie's high school did not have a baseball team, but he played basketball and football. He was such a good fullback in football that he considered concentrating on football and trying to win a college scholarship. But baseball kept beckoning, and when he was 16, his father earned him a tryout with the Black Barons.

Lorenzo "Piper" Davis, manager of the Black Barons, was so impressed with Willie's ability that he promptly signed him as an outfielder. As part of the agreement, Willie had to continue attending high school, and Willie's principal and the Barons' management worked out an agreement that permitted him to be excused from school when he was needed to play ball.

Shortly after Willie signed with the Black Barons, the Boston Braves offered Birmingham a contract for him. The Braves said they would pay the Black Barons $7,500 for Willie's contract and another $7,500 if he made good. The Chicago White Sox also were interested in signing Willie. But Willie could not sign with either team until after he graduated high school.

Meanwhile, a couple of scouts from the New York Giants were dispatched to check out the Barons' first baseman, Alonzo Perry. Instead, they came away with glowing reports of Mays. Ed Montague, one of the scouts, was so impressed with Mays that he called New York immediately.

"I saw a young kid of an outfielder I can't believe," said Montague. "He can run, hit to either field, and has a real good arm. Don't ask any questions. You've got to get this boy."

Montague was told not to leave Birmingham until he signed Mays. Montague offered the Barons $10,000 for Willie's contract, and Birmingham agreed, since it was more up-front money than the Braves had offered. On the day after Willie graduated from high school, the Giants offered him $2,000 to sign with them. However, Willie and his father said it wasn't enough money. They wanted $5,000. Montague immediately telephoned Giants owner Horace Stoneham, who agreed to the deal.

Willie was 19 when he reported to the Giants' Class B farm club in Trenton, New Jersey. By mid-season it was clear that Willie was too good for the league, but the Giants let him finish the season there. He was promoted to the Triple A affiliate in Minneapolis in 1951.

He starred immediately with Minneapolis. He hit practically everything pitched and fielded his position brilliantly. Giants manager Leo

Durocher got word about Mays' exploits and asked Stoneham to promote him to the big leagues.

"He's not ready for the majors," proclaimed Stoneham. "Anyway, he's due to go into the Army at any minute."

But the Giants hit a tailspin, losing 11 games in a row, and Durocher screamed again for Mays. At the time, Mays was hitting .477 at Minneapolis. Stoneham relented, but before bringing Mays up to the Giants, he took out an ad in the local papers and apologized to the Minneapolis fans for whisking Willie to the big leagues.

In his first few games with the Giants, Mays was a total flop. He managed only one hit, a home run off Braves' left-hander Warren Spahn, in his first 26 at-bats. One night after a game, Durocher entered the clubhouse and found Willie sitting in front of his locker, crying.

"What's the matter, son?" Durocher asked.

"Oh, Mister Leo," Willie said. "I can't do you any good. I can't get a hit. I can't win you any ball games. And I know you're gonna send me back to Minneapolis."

"Look, Willie," said Durocher, "this ball game's over. Tomorrow's another day. And don't you worry about me sending you back to Minneapolis. You're the best center fielder—you're the best ballplayer—I've ever seen. Now you go home and get a good night's sleep."

That was the turning point for Willie. The next night he singled in his first time at bat and tripled later in the game as the Giants beat the Pirates, 14-3. Sparked by Willie's all around play, the Giants staged one of the greatest comebacks in baseball history by rallying from 13 1/2 games behind in August to win the NL pennant. The Giants and Dodgers finished the regular season in a tie, and the Giants won a best-of-three play-off series on Bobby Thomson's dramatic three-run homer in the ninth inning of Game 3.

Willie hit .274 with 20 home runs to gain NL Rookie of the Year honors, but he missed most of 1952 and all of 1953 after being drafted into the Army. When he returned in 1954, he put together a season that made him a New York folk hero. Willie hit a league-leading .345 with 41 homers and 110 RBI to win Most Valuable Player honors and then led the Giants to a four-game sweep over the Indians in the World Series. Willie's catch of Wertz's drive saved Game 1, and he had four hits and knocked in three runs in the four games.

Moreover, he excited fans with his zestful play and endeared himself to them by playing stickball after home games with the kids on the streets of Harlem where he lived.

Willie spent three seasons under the watchful eye of Durocher, and the two men developed a mutual admiration society that continued long after both had left the game.

"Leo was good for me," said Willie. "He was a hard man for the veterans to play for. He'd chew out Monte Irvin and [Eddie] Stanky and [Alvin] Dark and [Whitey] Lockman and the rest. I was the only kid. Anytime I made a mistake, he'd sit me down and he'd say, 'Do you know what you did wrong?' If I said no, he'd explain it to me. He'd never holler. If I said yes, he'd say, 'Tell me what you did wrong,' and I'd tell him. Then he'd say, 'Okay, now that I'm sure you know what you did wrong, it'll be $200 the next time.'"

Durocher, who had been a teammate of Babe Ruth, never wavered from his claim that Mays was the best player in the history of the game.

"I have never seen a ballplayer with his all-around ability, his instinctive baseball genius," said Durocher. "There are only five things you can do to be great in baseball: hit, hit with power, run, field, and throw—and the minute I laid eyes on Willie, I knew he could do them all."

In 1955, Willie became the first New York player to top 50 homers in a season since Ruth, and his legend continued to grow until the Giants abandoned New York for the west coast, along with the Dodgers, following the 1957 season.

The change to San Francisco did wonders for the Giants' bank account, but it didn't do much for Willie's popularity. The San Francisco fans did not accept him at first. He had honed his reputation in New York, and San Francisco wanted its own hero. So Giants fans heaped their attention on rookie first baseman Orlando Cepeda. In the team's first year in California, the fans voted Cepeda the club's MVP.

Despite a league-leading 190 hits in 1960 and a four-homer game in 1961, Mays did not win over San Francisco fans until the pennant-winning season of 1962. That year, he showed his ability to perform in the clutch with a game-winning eighth-inning homer on the last day of the season that forced a tie with the Dodgers for first place, a pair of homers to win Game 1 of the playoffs, and a clutch single in the decisive Game 3.

Beginning in 1959, Mays drove in 100 runs in a season for eight consecutive seasons and won four home run crowns, including a career-high homer total of 52 in 1965. That year, he won the MVP for the second time, even though the Giants finished in second place.

Mays spent 16 seasons in San Francisco, 13 of them playing in Candlestick Park, where the wind played havoc with every fly ball. Former teammates of Mays insist that the swirling winds of Candlestick cost the Giants' slugger at least 100 career homers.

It was in Candlestick that Mays collected hit No. 3,000 on July 18, 1970. Mays, who was 39 at the time, stroked a second-inning single off Montreal's Mike Wegener for the historic hit.

One of the saddest moments in Stoneham's long career as owner of the Giants came in May of 1972, when he was forced to trade Mays because of financial troubles. He worked out a deal with the Mets and sent Willie back to end his career in New York, where it all began.

Mays's skills were declining and Stoneham could no longer keep him on the payroll. The Giants let him go for $100,000, a young pitcher named Charlie Williams, and a promise to take care of Mays. The Mets agreed to pay Mays $50,000 a year for the next 10 years, even if he could not play.

Willie homered in his first game with the Mets, but was used in only 88 games. In 1973, he got into 66 games and helped the team reach the World Series. In Game 2 of the Series, he embarrassed himself by falling on his face in pursuit of a line drive that fell for a hit and sparked a game-tying rally. But he redeemed himself with a single to put New York back ahead.

It was his last hurrah. Nagged by swollen knees, an inflamed shoulder, and bruised ribs, Mays retired after the 1973 season. In 1979, he was elected to the Hall of Fame in his first year of eligibility. But his election was not unanimous, prompting even Willie to shake his head in bewilderment. Indeed.

Eddie Murray

Ranking: 12th
Hit Total: 3,255

AP/Wide World Photos

I t was early in the 1987 season, and Eddie Murray, the slugging first baseman of the Baltimore Orioles, was off to a terrible start. As he stepped to the plate in the fourth inning of a May 8 game against the Chicago White Sox, he was batting only .202.

Murray had spent much of the afternoon taking extra batting practice, trying to iron out a few mechanical problems with his swing. For the first time in quite a while, he felt comfortable when he stepped up to the plate in the fourth inning against Chicago pitcher Jose DeLeon.

DeLeon was a right-handed pitcher, so Murray, a switch-hitter, was batting left-handed. He concentrated as DeLeon went into his windup. "Careful now, don't lunge. Keep those hands back, stay balanced." DeLeon delivered, and Murray stepped into the ball and swung with the fluid grace that had produced eight seasons of 25 or more home runs from 1977 to 1985. He connected solidly, and the ball cleared the fence for a home run.

Five innings later, the game was on the line as Murray again strode to the plate. The Orioles were trailing, 6-4, but had two runners on base with two outs in the ninth. Ray Searage, a left-hander, was now pitching for Chicago, so Murray stepped to the plate batting right-handed. Searage delivered the pitch and Murray hit the ball over the left-field fence for a three-run homer to give the Orioles a 7-6 victory.

The next night, Murray came to the plate batting right-handed against left-hander Joel McKeon in the fourth inning and delivered a two-run homer. In the sixth, he hit left-handed against right-hander Bob James and unloaded a solo homer. Murray's extraordinary hitting display made him the first player in baseball history to hit home runs from both sides of the plate in consecutive games.

Consistency from either side of the plate marked Eddie Murray's 18-year career in the major leagues. He hit 504 home runs, yet never more than 33 in any one season. He knocked in 1,917 runs, but his high was 124 RBI for a season. He had 3,255 hits, yet never had more than 186 in a season. He is one of only three players in history—Hank Aaron and Willie Mays are the others—to amass at least 3,000 hits and 500 home runs.

Murray was also known for his ability to deliver in the clutch. He hit 19 grand slams in his career—second only to Lou Gehrig's 23—and had an astonishing .399 batting average with the bases loaded. He was the most consistently productive switch-hitter in history, even though he did not become a switch-hitter until 1976, the year before he entered the majors.

"When a game is on the line, there's no one I'd rather see up there," former teammate and close friend Elrod Hendricks once said of Murray. "Even when he's not hitting, I want to see him because he'll rise to the occasion.

"It got to the point where you just expected it. You took it for granted."

Murray also played more games at first base (2,413) than any player in history, and his 1,865 assist total is the record for first basemen.

Yet, despite his many contributions on the field, Murray was an enigma off it. Although admired by his peers and charitable with his money, he could be surly and standoffish to the media.

In his final years with the New York Mets and Cleveland Indians, he earned a reputation as clubhouse poison and was accused of influencing younger players to adopt a negative attitude toward sportswriters.

Elrod Hendricks, a former Orioles player and coach, noted that Murray watched veteran Lee May's handling of the media when Murray arrived as a young rookie in 1977.

"The press always thought Lee was the big, bad wolf, and I think, subconsciously, Eddie copied a lot of things Lee did," Hendricks said.

Rich Murray, one of Eddie's brothers, said a story negatively portraying the Murray family that was written during the 1979 World Series was the catalyst for Eddie's poor relations with the media.

Whatever the reason, Murray was basically mistrustful of people he didn't know. He also disliked being referred to as a "superstar." One of the first things he did after becoming a baseball millionaire was to have a gold necklace made that read "JUST REGULAR."

"When somebody asks me what it's like to be a millionaire, I point to the necklace," said Murray in 1982 after signing a five-year, $5 million contract with the Orioles. "I like to think I'm the same as I was when I was playing ball for fun with my brothers back home in Los Angeles.

"If you're talking about real life—the things most people do—a million dollars a year is unimaginable, but it isn't in baseball today. I accept the fact that I'm lucky to be where I am. I also know that if I let the money bother me too much, I'll mess up the things that got it for me."

Strong family values are at the core of Eddie Clarence Murray's character. Born on February 24, 1956, Eddie was raised along with 11 brothers and sisters in a three-bedroom house in the Watts section of East Los Angeles, California. Eddie's father, Charles, worked for a rug company as a mechanic for more than 30 years, and the family always had plenty of food on the table. The first house the family owned had a large garage in the back, and Eddie and his brothers and sisters used to play a game they called "Strikeout" inside the garage.

The batter would stand at the back of the garage, and the pitcher would throw him a tennis ball. In order to get a hit, the batter had to drive the ball out of the garage through a door opening that was about 10 feet high, 12 feet wide and 20 feet away. A line drive straight up the middle was the only way to get a hit. It made Murray a line-drive hitter.

There also was a makeshift diamond in the backyard. The boys played a game using the tops of Crisco cans. The tops took the place of balls, and they were much tougher to hit.

"I don't know how it started, but I think it helped us a lot hitting curveballs later on," recalled Murray. "You could make that lid do wicked things if you were pitching, and you only had about a half inch of area to hit it."

The practice the boys got in the backyard paid off. Four of Eddie's brothers also played professional baseball. Charles was in the Houston organization, and Venice and Leon were in the San Francisco farm system. Younger brother Richie played briefly with the Giants and in the Indians' farm system.

The area of Los Angeles where Eddie grew up also was a hotbed of baseball talent. Eddie attended Locke High School, and among his high school teammates were future major leaguers Ozzie Smith and Darrell Jackson. Other major leaguers from the area included Bob Watson, who played with Charles Murray; George Hendrick, who played with Leon; and Reggie Smith, Bobby Tolan, Willie Crawford, Dave Nelson, Dock Ellis, Don Wilson, and Bobby Darwin.

Eddie was selected by the Orioles in the third round of the amateur draft in June 1973. He batted .287 at Bluefield, West Virginia, in the Appalachian League. In 1975, at Asheville, North Carolina, in the Southern League, the Orioles decided to make Murray a switch-hitter by teaching him to bat from the left side. His first time up left-handed, he hit a double.

Actually, batting left-handed was not that difficult for Murray. He had practiced hitting left-handed many times in the garage and in the backyard with his brothers. He and his brothers used to imitate the Dodgers' switch-hitting infield quartet of Wes Parker, Jim Lefebvre, Maury Wills, and Jim Gilliam.

"In the yard, we'd pretend to be different players in major league lineups and bat lefty or righty, depending on who they were," Murray said.

At spring training in 1976, Murray wasn't really in the Orioles' plans, but he impressed them with his batting skills. He was sent back to the minors but played so well that he was one of 15 players the Orioles protected in the expansion draft at the end of the season. After another good showing in the spring of 1977, Murray made the big club.

Since the Orioles already had Lee May at first base, Orioles' manager Earl Weaver used Murray mostly as a designated hitter in his rookie season. Instead of making things difficult for the rookie, May became Eddie's tutor. May not only taught Murray the finer points of hitting and fielding, but also how to fend off reporters with a fearsome stare.

The designated hitter role suited Murray well in his first season. Not having to worry about defense, he batted .283 with 27 home runs and 88 RBI to win the American League's Rookie of the Year award. He struck out 104 times in his first year but would never strike out 100 times in a season again, a remarkable achievement in the days of the free swingers.

In 1978, Eddie was the club's regular first baseman, and he proved to be as adept in the field as he was at the plate. He became the best in the league at making the 3-6-3 double play, and he had another fine year at the plate, batting .285 with 27 home runs and 95 RBI.

Driving in runs would become Murray's trademark throughout his career. During his 21 major league seasons, he knocked in more than 75 runs in 20 of them. Only in his last season, 1997, when he got into only 55 games did he fail to reach the 75-RBI mark.

The Orioles reached the World Series in Eddie's third year with the team. With Murray batting .295, hitting 25 homers, and knocking in 99 runs, the Orioles won the AL East pennant by eight games and beat the California Angels in the playoffs. The Orioles met the NL-champion Pittsburgh Pirates in the World Series and had a seemingly insurmountable three-games-to-one lead in the best-of-seven series. But Pittsburgh rallied to win the last three games and capture the championship.

Part of the reason for the Orioles' collapse was a terrible slump by Murray, who failed to get a hit in his last 21 at-bats. Eddie's family attributed the slump to an article written by New York columnist Dick Young that painted an ugly picture of the treatment Orioles' scout Ray Poitevint received from Eddie's brothers when he attempted to sign the 17-year-old in 1973.

In the article, Young wrote that Poitevint was cursed at, kicked out of Murray's house, and nearly run over by a car driven by one of the brothers. Poitevint said he had to make 17 trips to the Murray house before getting Eddie to sign a contract.

The article upset Eddie and his family badly. It contributed to Murray's wariness of the media during the remainder of his career.

Eddie didn't let his poor World Series performance affect his 1980 campaign, however. He had his best season, batting .300 with 32 homers and 116 RBI. With switch-hitting Ken Singleton knocking in 104 runs, the duo became only the second pair of switch-hitters on a team to drive in 100 runs apiece. (The Cardinals' Ted Simmons and Reggie Smith in 1974 were the first.)

After the 1980 season, Murray signed a five-year, $5 million contract to become baseball's youngest millionaire. Soon after signing the contract, Murray started "Project 33," named for his Orioles' uniform number. The program issued to inner-city youngsters 50 box seats for every Orioles home game. He also contributed money and time to a private school in Baltimore that helped dropouts complete their high school studies.

Murray might have had the best season of his career in 1981 if a players' strike had not wiped out two months of the season. As it was, Eddie hit 22 homers and knocked in 78 runs in 99 games. Beginning in 1982, Eddie hit a four-year stretch during which he knocked in at least 110 runs a season and hit a total of 125 homers.

In 1983, the Orioles won the world championship that eluded them in 1979. Murray hit .306 with 33 homers and 111 RBI during the regular season and batted .267 with one homer and three RBI as the Orioles beat the Chicago White Sox in the AL championship series. In the World Series, Eddie hit .250 with two homers and three RBI, but it was the hitting of his close friend, Rick Dempsey, that enabled the Orioles to defeat the NL-champion Philadelphia Phillies in five games. Dempsey, named the MVP of the Series, hit .385, and all five of his hits were for extra bases.

It was the last time Murray would get an opportunity to play in a World Series.

Murray put together two more strong seasons in 1984 and 1985, but in 1986, he suffered a hamstring injury that sent him to the disabled list for the first time in his career and limited him to 137 games.

Eddie hit .305 in 1986, but his home run total dropped to 17, and his RBI fell to 84, a drop of 40 from the previous year. The Orioles struggled through their first losing season in 20 years, and team owner Edward Bennett Williams unfairly blamed Murray for much of the team's problems. That did not sit well with the Orioles' slugger, who had been a loyal employee for his entire career. Moreover, he had played hurt for most of the '86 campaign and felt the front office should have praised him for that instead of berating him.

By the time spring training of 1987 rolled around, Murray was unhappy and wanted out of Baltimore. But, because he was now being paid more than $2 million a year, no team was willing to make a deal.

Matters grew worse between Murray and the Orioles. Although Eddie would hit 30 homers, including the memorable two homers in consecutive games from each side of the plate, and drive in 91 runs in 160 games, he batted a career-low .277. The Orioles had another horrid season, finishing 67-95 and in sixth place in the AL East. The fans took out their frustration on Murray and taunted him loudly. Finally, in August, Murray decided it was time to move on.

After the season, though, the Orioles fired general manager Hank Peters and hired energetic Roland Hemond to replace him. Murray felt at ease with Hemond immediately. When Williams also met with Murray to patch things up, Eddie decided to stay with Baltimore.

Murray's final year with Baltimore was 1988. He hit .284 with 28 homers and 84 RBI. But the team floundered again, and at the end of the season, Eddie was traded to the Los Angeles Dodgers, his hometown team. In spring training the next season, while Eddie was in the Dodgers' Vero Beach, Florida, camp, the Orioles announced they were retiring his number.

Eddie spent three seasons with the Dodgers and, once he learned NL pitchers, showed just as much consistency in the NL as he had in the AL. He batted only .247 in his first season with the Dodgers, but hit 20 homers and knocked in 88 runs. In 1990, he hit a lusty .330 with 26 homers and 95 RBI, and in 1991, he hit .260 with 19 homers and 96 RBI.

After the 1990 season, Murray signed as a free agent with the New York Mets and drove in 93 and 100 runs in his two seasons with them. He then played two and a half seasons with the Cleveland Indians before returning to Baltimore for 64 games in 1996. He closed out his career in 1997 with the Angels and Dodgers.

A certain Hall of Famer when he becomes eligible to enter baseball's shrine, Murray will be remembered for his extraordinary consistency and durability. He was a superstar despite his insistence to the contrary.

Nap Lajoie

Ranking: 13th
Hit Total: 3,242

AP/Wide World Photos

As Napoleon Lajoie stepped up to the plate against the Yankees on a summer day in 1910, pitcher Russ Ford took one look at the Cleveland slugger and decided he wanted no part of him. He would walk Lajoie intentionally.

On the fourth ball, Ford got the pitch a little too close to the plate, and Lajoie reached out with one hand and stroked the ball down the right-field line for a double.

On Lajoie's next trip to the plate, Ford decided on the same strategy, only this time he would make sure his pitches were nowhere near the strike zone. His fourth pitch was well off the plate, but once again, Lajoie plunked it into right field for another double.

Lajoie batted again late in the game, and Ford was determined to issue another intentional walk. But on the fourth pitch, Lajoie reached way over the plate and dumped the ball down the right-field line again for a third double. Three doubles on three intentional balls. That explains the artistry of Napoleon Lajoie as a hitter.

Want more evidence?

Cleveland was playing Boston in a game in 1912, and Lajoie stepped to the plate with his team trailing by four runs. Boston pitcher Buck O'Brien got two quick strikes on Lajoie, then decided to waste a pitch by throwing one at his head. The next sound he heard was the ball bouncing off the iron fence in center field, and two runs were in.

On Lajoie's next trip to the plate, O'Brien again worked the count to 0-2. At that point, Boston catcher Bill Carrigan walked to the mound.

"What are you going to do now?" Carrigan asked O'Brien.

"I'm throwing a pitch I never threw to him before, a round house curve," O'Brien said.

Lajoie hit the ball so hard that it caromed off the hip of Heinie Wagner, the Boston shortstop. Wagner immediately went to the mound to confront O'Brien. Wagner, O'Brien, and Carrigan shared an apartment together.

"I'm the captain of this club, Buck," said Wagner, "and if you throw that big Frenchman any more pitches like that, you won't get into the room to-night."

On his third trip to the plate, Lajoie hit one so hard down the third-base line that the ball split open the hand of third baseman Larry Gardner.

No one knows if O'Brien had to sleep in the clubhouse that night.

Napoleon Lajoie (pronounced LAH-joe-way) is considered by many baseball historians to be the prettiest hitter and the most graceful second baseman of his era. He was a big man physically, standing 6-foot-1 and weighing 195 pounds, and he hit the ball with such authority that infielders, especially third basemen, lived in fear of being seriously hurt by one of his line drives.

He collected 3,251 hits during his 21-year major league career, posted a .339 batting average, and won three American League batting titles. He was always among the league leaders in doubles and triples and twice led his league in home runs, hitting 10 for the Philadelphia Phillies of the National League during the 1897 season and 14 in 1901 for the Philadelphia Athletics of the American League.

As a fielder, he was known as the "Gliding Panther of Second Base" and led the AL in fielding percentage six times. Lajoie made plays effortlessly at second base, getting in front of balls on which other players would make acrobatic stops.

Lajoie's career coincided with that of Honus Wagner, the great Pittsburgh shortstop, and until Ty Cobb blossomed into stardom in 1907, the "French Devil,"—as some rivals used to call him—and the "Flying Dutchman"—as Wagner was known—were the big stars of the rival leagues.

Unlike Cobb, however, Lajoie was revered by teammates, opponents, and fans. A soft-spoken man who avoided confrontation, Lajoie was so popular that the Cleveland team, for whom he played for 12 seasons, was known as the Naps, in his honor.

Born on September 5, 1875, in Woonsocket, Rhode Island, of French-Canadian parents, Lajoie was driving a horse-drawn taxi in his hometown for $7.50 a week and playing baseball in his spare time when Charley Marston, the manager of a baseball team in Fall River, Massachusetts, offered him $100 a month to play for his team. Woonsocket and Fall River were adjoining towns. A contract was scribbled on the back of an envelope, and Lajoie signed quickly.

Lajoie was put in the outfield and immediately showed his prowess at the plate, posting a .429 batting average in 80 games. However, it was another outfielder on that team, Phil Geier, who attracted the interest of the Philadelphia Phillies of the National League, and they dispatched a scout to look him over and sign him.

The scout, Bill Nash, had no interest in Lajoie, despite his ability with the bat. Instead, Nash offered Marston $1,500 for Geier. Marston, perhaps fearing the scout would change his mind, offered to throw in Lajoie's contract, too, and so both young outfielders joined the Phillies.

It didn't take long for the Phillies to realize that Lajoie was the bargain, not Geier. Geier hit .232 in 17 games in 1896, while Lajoie hit .328 in 39 games. Geier lasted only a few years in the major leagues as a journeyman outfielder, compiling a .252 batting average in 342 games. Lajoie became a star almost immediately, batting .363 in his first full season of 1897. In 1898 he was installed as the Nationals' regular second baseman, a position where he would become known as "King Larry."

Lajoie hit .379 for the Phillies in 1899 and .346 in 1900. In 1900, the American League was formed, and league president Ban Johnson gave the Philadelphia franchise to Connie Mack. Mack then began raiding the NL for the best players. His first big deal was to sign Lajoie and two pitchers, Chick Fraser and Bill Bernard. Lajoie, making the maximum $2,400-a-year salary allowed by the NL, jumped at the chance of playing for more money.

Lajoie and Ed Delahanty, the two stars of the Phillies, each had signed a contract for the 1900 season, but under the table, the Phillies agreed to pay Delahanty, the 1898 batting champion, an extra $600. When Lajoie heard about it, he also demanded more money, but the best he could get was $200. He was angered over the difference between his pay and Delahanty's.

"Because I felt I had been cheated, I was determined to listen to any reasonable American League offer," Lajoie said. When the offer was made by Frank Hough, a sports editor acting as an agent for Connie Mack, Lajoie was astounded.

"Hough offered me $24,000 for four years," said Lajoie. "You can bet I signed in a hurry."

He made an immediate impact on the new league, capturing the AL's first batting title with a .422 mark. It turned out to be the highest average ever compiled by an American League player. That year, he also led the AL in runs, hits, doubles, homers, putouts at second base, and fielding percentage.

Although Lajoie officially batted .422 in 1901, his average for that season was carried as .405 for 36 years, beginning in 1918, because of a typographical error in the official record book of the era. The *Reach Guide,* covering the 1901 season, listed Lajoie with 543 times at bat and 220 hits for a .422 average. For the next 15 years, all record books carried the lofty mark for Lajoie, but in the winter of 1916, an inquisitive statistician re-checked the arithmetic and found that 220 hits in 543 times at bat figured out to .405 instead of .422.

Assuming there had been a mistake in division, rather than an error in printing in the original guide, the statistician arbitrarily cut Lajoie's average to .405 in listing the yearly batting records in the 1917 record books. As a result, Ty Cobb took over as the AL record-holder for highest batting average in a season with his .420 mark in 1911, a figure subsequently tied by George Sisler in 1922.

A self-effacing man, Lajoie did not complain when the change was made. A modern player would scream and holler if he were deprived of a single hit, but Lajoie quietly accepted what he later called "a mixup in my batting average."

It wasn't until 1953, when *The Sporting News* carried a story on Lajoie and mentioned the switch in figures, that the curiosity of a baseball fan named John C. Tattersall was aroused. The official records for 1901 had been destroyed, but Tattersall checked the daily box scores published in the *Boston Record* and the *Philadelphia Inquirer, Public Ledger,* and *Press.* His research found that Lajoie had collected 229 hits, *not* 220, in 1901, and he had, indeed, batted .422.

Tattersall's figures were confirmed by *The Sporting News,* which found in its issue of October 26, 1901, that Lajoie had been credited with 229 hits in the final AL averages. As corroborating evidence, the *Chicago Tribune* of October 21, 1901, also had listed Lajoie with 229 hits. Accordingly, in the *Official Baseball Guide* for 1954, Lajoie's average was restored to .422 for the 1901 season.

Only one player, Rogers Hornsby in 1922, had a better single-season average, with .424.

After the 1901 season, Mack induced two other Phillies stars, out-fielder Elmer Flick and pitcher Bill Duggleby, to jump to his team. The outraged Phillies sued for violation of the reserve clause in the standard player contract that bound a player to his team for life. A lower court found it illegal. But on appeal, the Pennsylvania Supreme Court reversed the finding of the lower court, upheld the reserve clause in favor of the Phillies, and ordered Lajoie and the other players to return to their old team.

However, only Fraser and Duggleby obeyed. Lajoie, Flick, and Bernard joined Cleveland of the AL. But so long as a National-American League war was on, it was necessary for the three men to forego playing all games with the Athletics in Philadelphia, since they were eligible for arrest once they entered Pennsylvania jurisdiction. The dispute ended upon the National League's acceptance of the American League in 1903.

Lajoie, Flick, and Bernard renewed interest in baseball in Cleveland. In fact, Cleveland was so excited about getting Lajoie that the team's nickname was changed from Blues to Napoleons in his honor.

He didn't disappoint, either. He hit .369 in 1902, but lost the batting title to his old Phillies' teammate Delahanty, who was now with Washington. Lajoie won the batting title in 1903 and 1904 and had the highest average in 1905, but a broken leg limited his play to 65 games.

In 1905, Lajoie became player/manager of Cleveland, and he served in that dual capacity until mid-season of 1909. His batting averages suffered during his managerial tenure. Twice during his four and a half seasons as manager, he hit below .300. Lajoie was not temperamentally suited to be a manager and was much too lenient with his players.

One night he stopped in the hotel room of one of his players, George Stovall, in an attempt to cheer him up. Stovall was brooding about the fact that he had been dropped down in the batting order. The more he brooded, the madder he got, and Lajoie's attempt to raise his spirits made him even more irritable. Finally, Stovall had enough and broke a wooden chair over Lajoie's head. Lajoie didn't even fine him.

"Why should I?" he said. "He's a good player, and he was a little upset."

Yet Lajoie may have cost his team the pennant in 1908 by not being lenient enough. Nig Clarke, the Cleveland catcher, was newly married and asked Lajoie for a day off so that he could go home. Lajoie refused. Clarke sulked and walked over to warm up pitcher Addie Joss. On the first pitch, he stuck out a finger and the ball broke it cleanly. With blood streaming from his hand, Clarke waved it defiantly in front of Lajoie.

"Now can I go home?" asked Clarke. He was out five weeks, and Cleveland lost the pennant to Detroit by half a game.

Lajoie realized that managing was affecting his ability to perform at his best as a player, so midway through the 1909 season, he quit as manager. Relieved of the pressures of leadership, Lajoie waged a battle with Ty Cobb for the 1910 batting title. Cobb won by the thinnest of margins in one of the most controversial races in history.

The Chalmers Automobile Co. offered a car to the batting leaders of each league that season. Sherry Magee of the Phillies easily won the NL race, but Lajoie and Cobb went down to the final weekend of the season for the AL crown.

Lajoie, affable and easy-going, was well-liked by everyone connected with baseball, while Cobb was detested by most people, including his own teammates. A number of Cobb's teammates on the Tigers were pulling for Lajoie to win the batting title and the car. Detroit ended the season with a four-game series in Chicago, while Cleveland had three games in St. Louis.

Cobb had four hits in seven at-bats in the first two games against the White Sox and then did not play in the third game. Lajoie had only one hit in four at-bats in his first game against the Browns. Cobb now had what appeared to be an insurmountable lead.

Apparently feeling he had won the championship, Cobb also decided to sit out the final game of the season. Cleveland was scheduled for a doubleheader with the Browns.

Jack O'Connor, a former catcher, was the manager of the Browns, and he concocted a plot, with the help of scout Harry Howell, to aid Lajoie in his bid to win the batting title. John "Red" Corriden, a rookie third baseman, was an unwitting participant in the scheme.

Each time Lajoie came to bat, O'Connor ordered Corriden to play very deep at third base, almost on the outfield grass. "He'll tear your head off with line drives," O'Connor warned the rookie.

Lajoie hit a triple in his first at-bat and also got an infield single. But on six other trips to the plate in the doubleheader, he beat out bunts for base hits. As a result of his 8-for-8 performance, Lajoie presumably had won the batting title. Only *The Sporting News* disagreed. The newspaper still had Cobb as the leader by .004.

Frank Navin, president of the Tigers, complained that Cobb had been given a raw deal, and league president Ban Johnson ordered an investigation of the circumstances surrounding Lajoie's safe bunts and summoned O'Connor, Howell, Corriden, and other players.

The inquiry revealed that the official scorer at St. Louis had received an anonymous note offering him a suit of clothes if he would give Lajoie the benefit of any doubt on any close plays.

In addition to his eight hits in eight official at-bats in the doubleheader, Lajoie had batted a ninth time and been credited with a sacrifice bunt, on which a run scored, even though third baseman Corriden had booted the ball. Johnson's investigation revealed that Howell had visited the press box and had attempted to persuade the official scorer to give Lajoie a ninth hit.

Corriden was absolved by Johnson of any wrongdoing, but St. Louis club owner Robert Lee Hedges fired O'Connor and Howell.

When the official AL batting averages were announced, they showed that *The Sporting News* was correct in naming Cobb as the winner. Cobb won the championship with a figure of .3848, compared to .3841 for Lajoie. The company awarding the car gave one to each of them.

The controversy resurfaced 71 years later, when Paul MacFarlane, a researcher for *The Sporting News,* rechecked the records, discovered that one of Cobb's games had been counted twice and that Lajoie actually should have won the batting title. The newspaper called for an official correction, but baseball commissioner Bowie Kuhn refused to honor the appeal for fear of setting off a chain reaction of revisionist history.

Following the 1910 campaign, Lajoie slowly began to fade as an everyday player. He played in only 90 games in 1911 because of injuries, and just 117 in 1912, although he kept his batting average above .360 for both seasons.

After hitting .335 in 1913, his average dropped to .258 in 1914, and the end was near. In 1915, Connie Mack began his breakup of the Athletics and sold his second baseman, Eddie Collins, to the Chicago White Sox. He purchased Lajoie from Cleveland to fill the gap at second, and Lajoie played his last two seasons with the A's, batting .280 in 1915 and .246 in 1916. In his last AL game, he helped Joe Bush win a no-hitter with a triple.

While Lajoie no longer could bat .300 in the major leagues, he did win one more batting title after going to the Toronto Maple Leafs in the International League in 1917 as player/manager. Lajoie, then 42, hit .380 to win the batting title and appeared in 151 of his team's 156 games. His hitting and all-around play were vital factors in Toronto's winning the pennant, the only time Lajoie ever played on a championship team.

Toronto sold Lajoie's contract to Brooklyn for $3,000, but Lajoie asked for permission to join Indianapolis as playing manager instead, and it was granted. However, the outbreak of World War I suspended play in mid-season, and Lajoie announced his retirement from the game in December of 1918.

Lajoie invested his baseball earnings wisely and lived comfortably in his later years. He was among the second group of players elected to the Hall of Fame in 1937.

Cal Ripken Jr.

Ranking: 14th
Hit Total: 3,184

AP/Wide World Photos

This was a different kind of streak for Cal Ripken Jr., the kind that doesn't get measured in the box scores or the record books, but in many ways goes a lot farther toward measuring the character of the man.

It was March of 1999 at the Baltimore Orioles' Fort Lauderdale, Florida, camp before an exhibition game. Only this was a little different day than normal because Ripken was not penciled into the Orioles' starting lineup.

Now, that happens about as often as it snows in Los Angeles. Ripken entered the 1999 season having played in a major league-record 2,478 consecutive regular-season games, and he had played in the first 13 games of the exhibition season.

Since this was an exhibition game, his consecutive-game streak was not in jeopardy of being broken. For the first four innings, Ripken sat in the dugout watching the game.

But in the top of the fifth, he emerged from the dugout and headed toward the fence near shallow right field. He turned over a water cooler, sat down, and started to sign autographs. Unlike the regular season, when fans are not allowed the opportunity to get close to the players and coaches, spring training provides a carefree and relaxed atmosphere and allows for much more interaction.

As he began signing every ball and piece of paper thrust in front of him, more and more people began to gather. Ripken did not disappoint any of them. Watching the game out of one eye, and protected by a security guard, he continued to sign for two hours.

When the game ended, Ripken headed toward the right-field corner. He had signed hundreds upon hundreds of autographs and accommodated almost every autograph seeker. As he began trotting back toward the Orioles dugout,

Ripken shook hands with and gave high-fives to the fans as they leaned over the fence to greet and catch a glance of him. He was applauded by those who remained. "Way to go, Cal," yelled an older gentleman.

Most of the fans who were able to get Ripken's autograph that day have long since forgotten the outcome of the game. But they will long remember Ripken's generosity. He very easily could have relaxed in the dugout for the entire game, but graciously spent his day off signing autographs. It's this magnanimous behavior that makes Ripken one of baseball's most revered stars.

There are very few players who give as much to the game of baseball as Calvin Edward Ripken, Jr. Three words stand out when describing Cal as both a player and a person—excellence, dependability, and consistency.

Quite simply, Cal has been one of the most remarkable athletes of his generation. He is one of only a handful of players to collect 3,000 hits and 400 home runs; he was twice voted the American League's Most Valuable Player; and he was one of the most sure-handed infielders ever to play the game.

But it was his ability to play practically every inning of every game over a 17-year period—all of it with the Orioles—that set him apart from other players. Before voluntarily removing himself from the starting lineup on September 20, 1999, Cal started a record 2,632 consecutive games. From June 5, 1982, through September 14, 1997, he played every inning of every game—an incredible 8,243 consecutive innings, the longest such streak in history.

Ripken's record is even more impressive because he played shortstop for most of that streak, baseball's most demanding position both physically and mentally. Lou Gehrig, by contrast, held the consecutive game record of 2,130 for more than half a century, but he played first base, considered the least demanding position.

Cal's willingness to take the field every day was remarkable, especially in an era of coast-to-coast travel and long-term guaranteed contracts that make it very easy to take a day off now and then. But from the time he was a youngster, Cal had an amazing appetite for learning as much as he could about baseball. And the best way to learn was to play as often as possible.

"You gotta play as many games as you can," Ripken once said. "Since there are so many possible plays, you can't get it all unless you're there every day. You can't get it from a book. You play games. And after you play so many games, experience so many different ground balls, runners, hitters, and situations, you learn to prepare for each hitter, each pitch, each option—even each potential injury."

Born in Havre de Grace, Maryland, on August 24, 1960, Cal was groomed to be a baseball player at an early age. His father, Cal Sr., spent more than 40 years in baseball as a player and manager at the minor league level and as a coach and manager at the major league level. Cal and his younger brother Billy, who also made the major leagues, both benefited greatly from their constant exposure to the game as youngsters.

"I learned very early that if I wanted to see my dad at all, I would have to go to the ballpark with him," said Cal. "I still wouldn't get to see him that much, but I'd ask questions on our drives to and from the ballpark. I liked those drives."

Much of Cal Sr.'s baseball career took him to out-of-the-way places such as Appleton, Wisconsin; Aberdeen, South Dakota; and Asheville, North Carolina. The family would accompany Cal Sr. to these towns during the summer, and Cal Jr. spent many days sitting in the stands at minor league games trying to learn the finer points of the game. He would read everything he could about baseball, and after the games would question his father about managerial strategies.

By the time he was 12, he began taking pregame infield and batting practice with his father's teams. In 1976, Cal Sr. was promoted to a major league coaching position with the Orioles. Cal Jr., now a high school student, frequented Baltimore's Memorial Stadium in between his own school and sandlot games, pitching batting practice, shagging flies, and picking up tips from Brooks Robinson, Mark Belanger, Ken Singleton, and other Orioles players. He also took a regular turn in the batting cage.

After games, Ripken would continue his practice of analyzing game strategies with his father.

"I was like a reporter," Cal said. "I'd review game charts and have all my questions ready. Why did this guy steal? Why didn't the catcher throw on this play? I would fire the questions at my dad. He'd tell me why everything happened. I'd question the players the next day. Why did you do that? What were you thinking?"

Although only 5-foot-7 in his freshman year at Aberdeen High School in Aberdeen, Maryland, Cal had grown to 6-4 by the time he was a senior, and baseball scouts began to take notice of him. A star pitcher and shortstop for his high school team, Cal batted .492 and posted a 7-2 record as a pitcher. Moreover, he struck out 100 batters in 60 innings and posted an earned run average of 0.70. He capped his high school career by striking out 17 and allowing just two hits in leading Aberdeen to the state championship.

Shortly after his graduation, Cal was selected by the Orioles in the second round of the 1978 free agent draft. Although he liked both pitcher and shortstop, he decided to concentrate on shortstop and was assigned to the Orioles' rookie league team in Bluefield, West Virginia.

He was hardly a phenom. He batted just .264 and was terrible in the field, committing a league-leading 33 errors. Some of his teammates were convinced that Cal had only made the team because of his father's connections, but he proved them wrong the next season by hitting .303 for the Orioles' A-level team in Miami.

The Orioles promoted Cal to Baltimore's AA team in Charlotte, North Carolina, before the end of the season, but he wasn't quite ready for the next level and batted just .180 in 61 at-bats. He opened the 1980 season at Charlotte and began to show real potential by batting .276 with 25 home runs.

Baltimore assigned him to its Triple A affiliate at Rochester in 1981, and he continued to develop as a power hitter by belting 23 homers and hitting .288 in 114 games. In August of 1981, Ripken was called up to the Orioles and got his first five major league hits in 39 at-bats.

Even though Ripken broke into professional baseball as a shortstop, the Orioles believed he was better suited to third base. So during the off-season, they traded their regular third baseman, Doug DeCinces, to the California Angels and handed the job to Cal.

Cal opened the 1982 season with a home run in his first at-bat, but by the end of April, he was batting only .117. Fearful that he might be sent back to the minors, he sought out his father for advice. His father told him to go "back to the basics," but it was some advice he got from Angels' slugger and future Hall of Famer Reggie Jackson that jump-started Ripken.

"Reggie told me he knew what I was going through because he'd been through it, too," said Ripken. "He told me to just be myself and everything would fall into place. After that, everything seemed to click."

For the rest of the 1982 season Ripken was a terror. He finished with 28 homers, 93 RBI and a .264 batting average, which was good enough to earn him Rookie of the Year honors. On July 1 of that season, Orioles manager Earl Weaver shifted Ripken to shortstop despite the concerns of some baseball observers who thought Cal was too big and slow to play such a demanding position.

But Weaver's hunch proved correct. Ripken shored up the Orioles' infield, and the club narrowly missed winning the AL East title, losing out to the Milwaukee Brewers on the final day of the season.

During spring training of 1983, Ripken informed the Orioles that he did not want to alternate between third base and shortstop. Joe Altobelli had taken over as manager of the team and informed Cal that he would play shortstop exclusively. Ripken responded with a spectacular season, batting .318 with 27 home runs and 102 RBI as the Orioles won the AL East title. Cal also led the league in runs scored (121) and doubles (47) and topped AL shortstops in assists (534), total chances (831), and double plays (131).

With Ripken batting .400, the Orioles beat the AL West-champion Chicago White Sox to win the pennant. Although Cal hit only .167 with one RBI in the World Series, the Orioles defeated the Philadelphia Phillies in five games for the championship.

In the voting for the AL MVP award, Ripken edged out teammate Eddie Murray to become the first player to win back-to-back Rookie of the Year and MVP honors.

Ripken put together another strong season in 1984, batting .304 with 27 homers, 86 RBI, and 103 runs scored. Defensively, he set an AL record for most assists by a shortstop and again led the league in total chances (906) and double plays (122). He also ranked first in putouts (297). But despite Ripken's fine play, the Orioles could do no better than fifth place in the AL East.

Cal's average slipped to .282 in 1985, but he hit 26 homers and knocked in 110 runs, establishing himself as one of baseball's best power-hitting shortstops of all time. He also led AL shortstops in double plays for the third straight year and in putouts for the second straight season.

Midway through the season, Earl Weaver returned as Orioles manager, but he failed to get the club moving, and the club finished the campaign in fourth place.

Weaver was at the helm again in 1986, and Cal responded by hitting .282 again with 25 homers and 81 RBI. He led the league in assists for the third time in four years, and he made only 13 errors in more than 700 chances. Still, the team floundered, and when the season ended, Weaver retired and Cal's father was named manager.

When spring training opened in 1987, there were three Ripkens wearing the Orioles uniform. Billy Ripken was a candidate for the starting second baseman's job, but Cal Sr. made it clear that he would not show any favoritism toward his two sons. Cal Sr. was true to his word, and Billy failed to make the Orioles' opening-day roster, although he was called up from the minors in mid-season. It made Cal Sr. the first manager in history to manage two of his sons.

Cal Jr., perhaps feeling the pressure of playing for his father, slumped to .252 at the plate, though he did hit 27 homers and drive in 98 runs. He also led the league's shortstops in assists for the fourth time in five years. The Orioles, though, endured a dismal season, finishing just 67-95 and in sixth place.

If 1987 was a nightmare, then 1988 was a sheer horror. The Orioles suffered through the worst start in baseball history, losing their first 21 games. Cal Sr. was fired after the first six losses, and not even his successor, former Orioles star Frank Robinson, could stop the bleeding. Even after Robinson took over, the team lost 15 more games in a row.

Cal finished the season with a .264 batting average, 23 home runs, and 81 RBI, but the Orioles finished with the worst record in the major leagues (54-107). After the season, Cal had the option of becoming a free agent, but decided to stay in Baltimore and signed a four-year deal worth $8.4 million.

Robinson guided the Orioles to a remarkable turnaround in 1989. The team led the East Division by 7 1/2 games at the All-Star break, only to falter in the second half and lose the division title to Toronto in the next-to-last game of the season. Ripken, though, had another solid season, hitting 21 homers and knocking in 93 runs. He became the first shortstop in history to have eight straight 20-homer seasons.

In the field, he committed only eight errors and led AL shortstops in putouts, assists, total chances, and double plays.

Ripken achieved a baseball milestone in 1990 when he played in his 1,308th consecutive game to pass Everett Scott and move into second place on the all-time consecutive-game list. He also broke Scott's record for consecutive games played at one position.

"It wasn't a goal coming into the big leagues that I wouldn't miss a game," Ripken said. "You just try to prepare yourself each and every day and go out there."

That same year, Ripken accomplished an amazing feat. He committed only three errors, a record for shortstops, and went 95 games without an error. A year later, he earned his second AL MVP award by hitting .323 with 34 homers and 114 RBI despite a sixth-place finish by the Orioles.

Ripken earned a special place in baseball history in 1995 when he surpassed Lou Gehrig's mark for consecutive games, a record that had stood for 55 years. He continued to play every game until September 20, 1998, when he asked Orioles manager Ray Miller to take him out of the lineup 30 minutes before a game with the New York Yankees. The streak ended at 2,632 games.

A year before, his streak of 15 years as the Orioles' everyday shortstop had ended when he was moved back to third. By early 1999 the strain of playing day in and day out every season began to affect Ripken physically. For the first time in his career he went on the disabled list, with a sore back. He underwent surgery on Sept. 24, 1999, to relieve pressure on the nerve roots.

Ripken recovered in time for spring training 2000 and joined baseball's elite 3,000 hit club on Saturday, April 15, with a base hit off reliever Hector Carrasco of the Minnesota Twins at the Metrodome in Minneapolis.

Although his baseball feats will eventually land him in the Hall of Fame, he will be remembered just as much in Baltimore for his many charitable works for the community. Cal and his wife, Kelly, established the Cal Ripken, Jr., Foundation in 1992 to expand upon the Ripkens' charitable and personal giving. Cal has been the recipient of both Major League Baseball's Bart Giamatti Caring Award and the Roberto Clemente Award in recognition of his charitable efforts.

It's a streak he plans on continuing long after his playing days are over.

Editor's note:
After 21 seasons with the Baltimore Orioles, baseball's Iron Man retired in 2001. He still holds the MBL record for most consecutive games played (2,632) and is one of only a handful of players to collect over 400 home runs. A 19-time All-Star, Rikpen Jr. was elected to the Baseball Hall of Fame in 2007 with the third-highest voting average in Hall of Fame history (98.53).

George Brett

Ranking: 15th
Hit Total: 3,154

AP/Wide World Photos

Denny Matthews, one of the announcers for the Kansas City Royals, had rented some early-morning ice time at a Kansas City rink and had coaxed some of the Royals' players to participate in some noncontact hockey.

When Matthews showed up at the rink at 6:30 am., one of the first players to arrive was George Brett, the team's superstar third baseman. Brett, a native of California, had never been on skates before, but had heard some teammates talking about the game and wanted to participate. On a road trip to Toronto, he had purchased some skates, and now he was ready to try them out.

When Matthews saw Brett, he began to laugh.

Brett began to burn.

"What are you laughing at?" Brett asked. "I've got $10 that says I can beat you from one end of the rink to the other."

"Hey, you're from California, and you don't even know how to skate," Matthews replied.

"Get up the money," Brett responded.

Brett laced on his skates and was champing at the bit. Matthews was an accomplished skater, and Brett was skating for the first time in his life. It didn't matter. Brett was determined he could beat Matthews.

The two men took off, with the graceful Matthews holding only a slight lead over the lumbering Brett. It remained that way until the end, with Matthews barely beating Brett, who finished the race on his ankles.

It was a perfect example of the competitive spirit that drove George Brett to a Hall of Fame career.

"He's a competitive guy, and it doesn't make any difference what is; if he wants something, he'll go after it," said Charley Lau, the man who taught Brett how to hit.

"George will try to out-arm wrestle you, out drink you, beat you at pool, anything, as long as there is a stake," said one of Brett's friends.

———————

George Howard Brett came about his competitive nature quite naturally. He was the product of a very demanding father and one of four brothers who, when they weren't fighting with each other, were trying to outwit, outhustle, or outplay opponents on the baseball diamonds of El Segundo, California.

George was the youngest of the four and, ironically, was the one their father, Jack Brett, thought would amount to the least. It was the second born, Ken, upon whom most of the attention was lavished. Ken was the star athlete in the family as a youngster, and it was Jack's dream that Ken would replace Mickey Mantle in center field for the New York Yankees.

He never did, but he did spend 14 seasons in the major leagues as a pitcher with 10 different teams and distinguished himself as one of the game's best-hitting pitchers.

Brothers John and Bobby also made it into professional baseball, although their careers ended because of injuries in the low minors. And George? Well, he surprised them all. Not in his father's wildest dreams, nor those of anyone else in El Segundo, was George going to achieve stardom in the major leagues.

But let the records speak for themselves. George played 21 seasons in the major leagues, all of them with the Royals, and compiled a lifetime batting average of .305 that included three batting titles and 3,154 hits. He led the American League in doubles twice, in triples three times, and in slugging percentage three times. He hit 20 or more home runs in eight seasons and topped the 100-RBI, 100-run marks on four occasions each.

"People say that I always knew George was going to make it, but that isn't true," said Jack Brett. "I was pretty sure Ken would; I neglected George."

George became more than just a great hitter. He was the inspirational soul of a Kansas City team that won six AL West Division titles, two AL pennants, and a World Series championship from 1976 to 1985.

"George was the Kansas City Royals," said former teammate Jamie Quirk. "We had some great players, but George was our heart and soul."

Brett played the game hard. His statistics may have been even greater had not his aggressive style of play landed him on the disabled list 10 times. He missed more the 400 games because of various injuries.

Born on May 15, 1953, in Glen Dale, West Virginia, Brett grew up in California in a giant shadow cast by his brother Ken. It was Ken Brett the baseball scouts came to see in high school.

"With Ken, you always knew he was going to be a star," said Bobby Brett. "He wasn't just the best guy on the team. He was always the best guy in the league by far. He was Southern California Player of the Year two times in his division. He was a superstar in a competitive hotbed of baseball."

Ken, five years older than George, was drafted as a pitcher by the St. Louis Cardinals following his senior year in high school and pitched in a World Series when he was 19. A year later, he was in the Army, and upon his return to the major leagues, he tried to make up for lost time and hurt his arm in spring training. He was never the same again. Although he pitched 14 seasons in the majors, he never won more than 13 games in a season. His biggest claim to fame is a record he holds for pitchers by hitting a home run in four successive games.

George's start in baseball was far less auspicious. He developed an early interest in baseball by following his brother around. But, whereas Ken possessed an athletic build and was a star from the time he was a youngster, George was only 5-foot-1 and 105 pounds when he was in ninth grade. The JV coach wanted to cut him from the team, but the varsity coach, who had known George since he was in grade school, overruled him. By the time George was a junior, he had filled out and was a starter at shortstop on the varsity.

He did possess one talent that no one else in the family could match. George was ambidextrous and once pitched in a high school game using both hands.

George's high school team was extraordinary. The team went 33-2 in his senior year, and six players went on to play professionally. George was only one of a handful of good players. The best was a left-handed pitcher named Scott McGregor, who went on to become a 20-game winner for the Baltimore Orioles.

Perhaps it was his bloodlines or the fact that his team did so well that George was selected in the second round of the free-agent draft by the Royals. He hit only .351 in his senior year, which is not terrific by high school standards. He also was not the highly competitive athlete at the time that he would later become.

"A lot of scouts would come to our games because the school had a reputation for producing good teams," said Brett. "The scouts were all the time being told, 'See that guy? That's Ken Brett's brother.'"

All four boys were driven hard by their father, a strict disciplinarian and perfectionist. George, though, seemed to get the worst of it. Once, after George struck out twice in a game, his father refused to talk to him all the way home in the car.

"I remember I got out of the car in my uniform, my head hanging," said George, "and the next thing I felt was a foot coming right up my behind. For embarrassing the family."

Even into his big-league career, George always suffered his father's criticisms.

"If I hit .329, my father says I should hit .350," George said during the 1980 season. "If I hit 23 homers, he thinks I should've hit 30. He's always pushing—always."

Scott McGregor remembers how irritable Jack Brett would get if George had a bad game.

"He was hard on his kids, very intense," said McGregor. "But my dad pushed me, too. That's the way of life in El Segundo."

It was assumed, after George signed a professional contract, that his baseball life would end in the minors, as it had for his brothers John and Bobby. And, indeed, he did not get off to a very good start. He spent three seasons in the minors and never hit over .300.

When George finally got to the big leagues in 1974, he was fortunate to come under the tutelage of batting coach Charley Lau. George had a big swing and was strictly a pull hitter. Lau taught him to use the whole field. He moved him away from the plate, closed his stance and taught him to keep the bat parallel with the ground.

The results were dramatic. Playing regularly at third base, George was hitting .289 late in the season when Lau was abruptly fired by Royals manager Jack McKeon. George was devastated and did not get another hit for the rest of the season and finished at .282.

Lau, however, returned as batting coach the next year when Whitey Herzog replaced McKeon as manager. Brett immediately responded to Lau by hitting .308. The next year, he won his first batting title, with a .333 average, but the result was controversial.

Brett, teammate Hal McRae, and Minnesota's Rod Carew went into the last day of the 1976 season in almost a dead heat for the batting title. During the game, Minnesota outfielder Steve Brye misjudged a ball hit by Brett, and the official scorer ruled it a hit. Brett won the batting title by a percentage point over McRae, who angrily charged that the ball had been deliberately misplayed so that Brett would win the batting title.

"I'm not saying that I'd have been just as happy if Hal had won instead of me, but I sure did hate the way it happened," said Brett. Brett refused to watch a replay of the hit. "A good friend was hurting," he said.

The Royals won the AL West title for the first time in 1976, but they lost to the New York Yankees in a five-game AL Championship Series. It would be the first of four battles between the two teams over a five-year period.

In 1977, Brett showed signs of becoming a power hitter. He batted .312 with 22 homers (doubling his previous high), knocked in 88 runs, and scored more than 100 (105) for the first time. The Royals won the AL West title again, but were beaten for the second straight year by the Yankees in a five-game AL Championship Series.

The Royals won the AL West crown again in 1978, even though Brett was limited to 128 games because of injuries. George hit three home runs in Game 3 of the AL Championship Series, but the Royals lost to the Yankees again, this time in four games. Following the season, Lau was fired as batting coach.

"I guess what happened," said Brett, "is that they started worrying that we were all hitting for average, but not utilizing our power. Like that year, I hit nine home runs, Al Cowens had just five, and Hal McRae's home run production fell off, too."

Others felt, however, that Lau was receiving too much credit for the Royals' success and that this irked Herzog, as it did his predecessor, McKeon.

George found out that he didn't need Lau anymore to stay focused. In 1979, George hit .329 with 23 homers, 107 RBI, and 119 runs scored. He was now an established star, but it was only a foreshadowing of what was to come in 1980.

That year, George made a run at the .400 mark, a figure that had last been achieved in 1941 when Ted Williams hit .406. Although limited to 117 games because of injuries, George finished at .390 with 23 homers and 118 RBI—better than an RBI per game—and led the Royals to the AL West championship. At one stretch of the season, he hit in 30 consecutive games. He was named the league's Most Valuable Player.

"He's probably the best ballplayer I've ever seen in my life," said Bill White, a former big league all-star who became an announcer, "but what's more significant to me is that I've never seen anyone, anywhere, who played so damned hard every day, day in and day out. He plays every game like it's the seventh game of the World Series."

Brett's best moment came in the AL Championship Series, when he homered off Rich Gossage in the seventh inning of Game 3 to give the Royals a three-game sweep of the Yankees for the first pennant in franchise history. George hit .375 in the World Series, but the Royals lost to the Philadelphia Phillies in six games.

A players' strike shortened the 1981 season, and though the Royals won half of it, they lost to the Oakland A's in the first round of playoffs to determine the AL West champion. Brett hit .314—a drop of 76 points from the previous season—and he managed only six home runs and 43 RBI.

One of the more bizarre moments in Brett's career occurred on July 24, 1983, at Yankee Stadium. Brett, who never wore batting gloves but instead covered the handle of his bat with pine tar to improve his grip, delivered a dramatic two-run homer off Gossage in the top of the ninth inning to give Kansas City a 5-4 lead, But Yankees manager Billy Martin quickly informed plate umpire Joe Brinkman that the pine tar on Brett's bat extended more than the allowable 18 inches. Brinkman concurred and disallowed the home run, giving the Yankees a 4-3 victory,

Brett came charging out of the dugout, wild-eyed, and had to be restrained from attacking Brinkman. The Royals filed a protest, and AL president Lee MacPhail, saying the pine tar rule was too vague, overruled the umpires and said that Brett's homer counted and that the game should be resumed.

The Yankees filed a series of legal countermoves, but when those efforts to reverse MacPhail's decision failed, the teams took the field again on August 18—originally an off-day for both teams—to resume play from the moment of Brett's homer. There were only 1,245 people in the stands, and the Yankees fielded a team that had pitcher Ron Guidry in center field and left-handed Don Mattingly, normally a first baseman, at second base.

As soon as the game got under way, George Frazier, the Yankee pitcher, threw to first base on an appeal play; the Yankees were claiming that Brett failed to touch first on his home run trot 25 days earlier. First-base umpire Tim Welke signaled safe. The Yankees tried the same thing at second base. When second-base umpire Dave Phillips gave the safe signal, Martin came out of the Yankees' dugout to argue. He wanted to know how Phillips could possibly know if Brett touched second base when he was umpiring a game in Seattle on July 24.

Phillips then produced a notarized letter from the original umpiring crew saying that both Brett and U.L. Washington, who was on base at the time, had touched all the bases. MacPhail and his assistant, Bob Fishel, had anticipated the appeal and requested that Brinkman's umpiring crew notarize a letter.

When the game finally resumed, it took 12 minutes to complete, with Kansas City holding on to the 5-4 victory.

Two years later, Brett led the Royals to their first world championship. With Brett batting .335, hitting 30 homers, and knocking in 112 runs, the Royals won the AL West title. In the AL Championship Series, George was the MVP, as the Royals came from behind to defeat the Toronto Blue Jays in five games. The Royals posted another comeback in the World Series, rallying from a three-games-to-one deficit to beat their intrastate rivals, the St. Louis Cardinals. Although Brett would play eight more seasons, it would be his last trip to the postseason.

Brett won his third and final batting crown in 1990, becoming the only player ever to win a batting title in three different decades. His greatest personal moment came on October 1, 1992, when, at the age of 39, he collected four hits against the California Angels to reach the 3,000-hit plateau. His 3,000th hit was a single off rookie reliever Tim Fortugno that hit the dirt in front of second baseman Ken Oberkfell and took a big hop over his shoulder into right field.

Brett played one more season, then retired. In 1998, he was elected to the Hall of Fame in his first year of eligibility. Brett received 98.19 percent of the vote, the fourth-highest total in history.

Paul Waner

Ranking: 16th
Hit Total: 3,152

Courtesy of Pittsburgh Pirates

G abby Street knew a hangover when he saw one, and he could smell this one from 90 feet away. It was a hot, early-summer day in 1932 at Sportsman's Park in St. Louis, and Pittsburgh outfielder Paul Waner, his head spinning and his eyes squinting painfully in the bright sunshine, had that look of someone who had gone to bat against John Barleycorn once too often the previous evening.

"Had a rough night, Paul?" inquired Street, the manager of the Cardinals, as the two men passed each other on the field prior to the game.

"Rough night?" Waner moaned, the stench of liquor emanating from the pores on his sweating brow. "What a host that Meine is."

Waner was referring to Heinie Meine, a Pittsburgh pitcher who operated a bar in a St. Louis community called Luxembourg. Waner, whose reputation as a drinker was as legendary as his batting stroke, had spent the night tossing down whiskey with Meine and a few of his cronies.

"Who's pitching for you today?" Waner inquired.

"Dean," said Street.

"Oh, no, not Diz," complained Waner. "Tell him to take it easy on old Paul, will you, Sarge?"

Gabby Street, the former World War I sergeant, patted the Pittsburgh player patronizingly on the back and said, "Sure, Paul, sure."

Heading back to the St. Louis dugout, Street smiled. "This is one day that little so-and-so won't bother us," he said to himself.

All Paul Waner did that day was hit a record-tying four doubles off one of the greatest pitchers who ever lived.

When Paul Glee Waner's parents named him back in Harrah, Oklahoma, in 1903, they didn't realize how appropriate that middle name was. Fun was definitely Paul Waner's middle name and the code by which he lived his life. He liked late hours, liquor. and friendly company.

Honus Wagner, the Pirates' Hall of Fame shortstop, once was asked to describe Paul Waner.

"He was a lowball hitter and a high ball drinker," Wagner said with a twinkle in his eye.

Ah, but what a hitter!

Although only 5-foot-8 1/2 and never weighing more than 153 pounds, Waner collected 3,152 hits over a 20-year career. He actually had 3,153 hits, but he refused to accept an official scorer's decision awarding him hit No. 3,000 and made him change it to an error. Waner wanted a clean hit for the historic occasion.

A left-handed hitter who stood deep in the batter's box, Waner had 200 or more hits in a season eight times and won three National League batting titles. He batted over .300 for 12 straight seasons (1926-37), reaching a high of .380 in 1927. He had a lifetime batting average of .333.

Waner was a line-drive hitter who hit sharply to all fields, but to say that he had a keen batting eye is not quite accurate. He actually was very nearsighted but preferred to hit without eyeglasses because he could see the ball better that way.

"When I wear glasses, the pitch looks as big as a baseball," he said. "But when I don't wear glasses, it looks as big as a grapefruit." He finally did succumb to wearing glasses, but not until very late in his career.

Despite his size, Waner was not strictly a singles hitter. He paced the NL in doubles twice, triples twice, and RBI once. He also scored 100 or more runs in a season nine times, and led the league twice in that department.

Waner also was an excellent outfielder. He was one of the fastest runners in the NL and possessed a powerful throwing arm. He threw out 31 base runners one season to lead the league in assists.

Waner's younger brother, Lloyd, was also an accomplished hitter, with a .316 lifetime mark for 18 major league campaigns. Lloyd hit .300 or better in 11 seasons. With Lloyd leading off and Paul batting third, they played together with the Pirates for 14 years, until 1940, when they were both traded.

The brothers also bore two of the most colorful nicknames in baseball lore, "Little Poison" for Lloyd and "Big Poison" for Paul. Those monikers were not applied because of the danger the duo posed to enemy pitchers, although that was considerable, but because of a Brooklyn fan's reference to them as "little person" and "big person." In Brooklynese, "person" comes out sounding like "poison."

"Every time you look up, those Waner boys are on base. It's always the little poison on thoid and the big poison on foist."

The quote is perhaps apocryphal, but it is supported by facts. The Waners spelled trouble for every NL pitcher. In Lloyd's rookie season of 1927, when the Pirates won the pennant, the two combined for 460 hits, with Paul's 237 and .380 average earning him the Most Valuable Player award.

As great a player as Paul Waner was, however, he was as well known for his nighttime adventures as he was for his batting prowess. When Pie Traynor, the Pirates' great third baseman, became manager of the team in the 1930s, he suggested to Waner that he might bat .400 if he would give up hard liquor and switch to something a little less potent, like beer.

Waner agreed, but the first time around the league, he was batting only .240. When the Pirates hit New York, the two men went out for a walk and happened by a bar. They walked in, and the bartender inquired, "What'll you have, gents?"

Traynor said he'd have a beer.

"Me, too," said Waner.

"He will like hell," said Traynor. "Give him a shot of whiskey." Traynor said Waner began hitting like his old self for the remainder of the season.

Then there was the time Waner stayed out all night carousing and showed up at the team's hotel in Chicago at noon, just as the rest of his teammates were leaving for Wrigley Field for an afternoon game with the Cubs. So that manager George Gibson would not see Waner, some of his teammates promptly rushed him out the door and into a taxi.

When the cab stopped for a red light near Wrigley Field, Waner jumped out and went into a restaurant.

"Gotta get a couple of hamburgers, I haven't had breakfast," Waner said.

The place smelled of onions, and after downing a couple of onion-soaked hamburgers, Waner went to the ballpark. He was still bleary-eyed from his night on the town, however, and in the first inning, he misjudged a fly ball so badly that center fielder Freddy Lindstrom had to retrieve it in right field.

Waner also was helpless at the plate. The Pirates were trailing by a run when Waner stepped to the plate in the ninth inning with runners on second and third. One of the Pirates' players suggested to Lindstrom that they inform Gibson about Waner's condition.

"Now, after we've connived and contrived all day to fool the man?!" said Lindstrom. "Hell, he'll fine us all. We've gone this far. Let's go all the way."

So Waner stepped to the plate against fastballing Guy Bush. Bush's first pitch jammed Waner, but he managed to get his bat on it and poke a little blooper just over third base. The ball fell in for a hit, and two runs scored. The Pirates hung on for the victory, and later in the jubilant clubhouse, Gibson walked over, put his arm around Waner, and addressed the rest of his ball club.

"Maybe the rest of you guys would be great hitters like Waner—if you ate onions."

Paul Glee Waner was born on a farm near Harrah, Oklahoma, on April 16, 1903. His parents were German, and his father was a prosperous farmer. Paul attended grammar school in Harrah but moved to Oklahoma City for high school, where he played first base and outfield for the baseball team.

After high school, Paul attended East Central State Teachers' College in Ada, Oklahoma, for two years. He gave some thought to becoming a teacher, but while he was playing college and independent ball in Oklahoma, he caught the eye of a part-time scout working for the San Francisco Seals. Waner joined the Seals in 1923 and showed an aptitude for batting from the start. As a 20-year-old rookie, he batted .369 in 112 games. He hit .356 in 1924, his first full season in the Pacific Coast League, and followed that with a league-leading .401 campaign. The league expanded to 174 games that year, and Waner had 280 hits, including 75 doubles.

Most of the big-league clubs had scouts trailing Waner that season, but the San Francisco management was particularly interested in a package deal that included Waner and a hotshot shortstop named Hal Rhyne.

The Pirates were coming off a world championship season, and team owner Barney Dreyfuss, prodded by scout Joe Devine, outbid his rivals and purchased Waner and Rhyne. Rhyne never lived up to the potential he had shown in the PCL, but Waner was an immediate hit. He batted .336 in his rookie season in the NL in 1926.

During that season, a scout for the New York Giants was following the Pirates and reporting his findings back to Giants' manager John McGraw.

"That little punk don't even know how to put on a uniform," the scout told McGraw.

Later that season, when Waner had practically singlehandedly torn the Giants apart in a series, McGraw fired the scout.

"That little punk don't know how to put on a uniform, but he's removed three of my pitchers with line drives this week," said McGraw. "I'm glad you did not scout Christy Mathewson."

Following the 1926 season, Dreyfuss called Waner into his office to discuss contract terms for the 1927 season.

"You're a pretty good hitter, young man," said Dreyfuss, "but you can't bunt and you can't come in for a ball."

"Neither can Babe Ruth, but he gets $70,000," said Paul.

"You don't think you're Babe Ruth, do you?" snapped Dreyfuss.

"No, but I think I'm pretty good," Paul replied. Dreyfuss agreed and doubled Paul's salary.

Paul earned his money in 1927. Joined by his brother, Lloyd, Paul won the league batting title, drove in 131 runs, and helped the Pirates win the NL pennant.

"I just couldn't do anything wrong that season," said Paul. "It was only necessary for me to poke my bat at the ball and hits would explode to all fields. It surely was fun. I was hitting right-handers and southpaws with equal ease."

The Pirates met the powerful New York Yankees, led by Ruth and Lou Gehrig, in the 1927 World Series and were swept in four games. A myth grew as years passed that the '27 Yankees, recognized as perhaps the greatest team ever, crushed the Pirates in the World Series. But two of the Pirates' losses were caused by a bad-hop grounder that hit the second baseman in the chest, resulting in a 5-4 defeat, and a ninth-inning passed ball that snapped a 3-3 tie.

When Ruth saw the Waner brothers for the first time prior to the Series, he was surprised. "Why, they're just kids," he said. "If I was that little, I'd be afraid of getting hurt." Lloyd hit .400 in the Series and Paul batted .333.

"We weren't overpowered," said Paul. "There were only two home runs hit in the Series, both by Babe Ruth. One of them was off a second-string pitcher, Mike Cvengros, after a game had already been lost. We weren't disgraced."

The 1927 season was Paul's second year in the big leagues and Lloyd's first. It was the only time they would play in a World Series during their Hall of Fame careers.

"Even though Pittsburgh lost four straight to the Yankees, that Series was a great event for the Waner boys," Paul reminisced years later. "Remember, Lloyd was only 21, and I 14; we both were just a few years off the farm and playing in the nation's top sporting event. It all seemed part of a big dream. Perhaps if I had known that I was to play in only one

World Series in a 20-year big-league career, it would have been even more of a thrill."

Waner was one of the few hitters who would deliberately make himself look bad swinging at a certain pitch. He did it so that the pitcher would think he could get Waner out with that same pitch at any time. Then, in a crucial situation when the pitcher would deliver his "out" pitch, Waner would invariably crush it for a hit.

The Pirates dropped to fourth place in 1928, but Paul hit .370 to finish second to Rogers Hornsby in the batting race. He then hit .336, .363, .323, .341, and .309 before winning his second batting title in 1934 with a .362 average. Two years later, he would hit .373 to win his third and final batting title.

Pittsburgh made only one more serious run at the pennant during Paul's career. It came in 1938 when Pittsburgh blew a seven-game lead in September and lost by two games to the Cubs. Paul hit only .280 that season and shouldered the blame for the Pirates' late-season collapse.

Paul climbed back to .328 in 1939, but the end of his career was in sight. After the 1940 season, he was released by the Pirates and was picked up by the Boston Braves. It was with Boston in 1942 that he joined baseball's 3,000 hit club—twice.

He opened the season with 2,956 hits, but early in the campaign, he was robbed of a hit by an official scorer, who ruled an apparent infield single an error.

Said Waner: "When I returned to the bench, someone said: 'Too bad, Paul. That would have been your 2,999th.' I shook my head. 'I don't want it tainted,' I answered."

It was now mid-June, and Waner had 2,999 hits but had gone 25 games without one. In the first game of a doubleheader, Tommy Holmes was a base runner on first and Waner at bat when the Braves put the hit-and-run on. Holmes broke for second on the pitch just as Eddie Joost, the Cincinnati Reds' shortstop, started over to cover the bag. Paul hit the ball to the spot Joost had vacated, and Joost immediately backtracked and got his glove on the ball but couldn't hold it.

In the press box, the official scorer lifted a forefinger to indicate a hit. Beans Reardon, the umpire, retrieved the ball and trotted to first base with the souvenir. Waner, however, was standing on the bag shaking his head emphatically and shouting, "No, no, no!" at the press box. Reluctantly, the scorer reversed the decision. Waner then apologized to Joost, a 26-year-old who was in his second full big-league season.

"I'm sorry to see you get the error, kid, but I wanted it to be one I could be proud of," Waner said.

Waner got his 3,000th hit two days later against his old Pittsburgh club, singling sharply to left off Rip Sewell. Typically for Waner, he threw a party that night for the players and invited the press and the Braves' front office, too.

Paul was back with the Dodgers in 1943 and hit .311 for them in 82 games, but they released him in early September 1944. With a chance to win the 1944 pennant, Joe McCarthy, then manager of the Yankees, got Waner near the end of that war season. Paul played in nine games for the Yankees but got only one hit in seven at-bats.

He accompanied the Yankees on their 1945 spring training trip to Atlantic City, but was released on May 3 after managing just one pinch-hit appearance.

Paul tried to make a fresh start in the minors as player/manager of the Miami team of the Florida International League in 1946, but he did not last the season. He closed his playing career by hitting .325 for Miami in 62 games.

After his playing career, Paul became a batting coach with the Boston Red Sox during spring training and taught the art of hitting to batters on numerous other teams. In 1952, he was elected to the Baseball Hall of Fame.

Robin Yount

Ranking: 17th
Hit Total: 3,142

SPI Archives

Robin Yount was going at full speed. As he approached a takeoff spot, he launched into the air and came full force to the ground as dust rose in the air on all sides of him. He let go with a big smile and knew he had made it. Then he did it again...and again...and again.

This wasn't Robin Yount, the ballplayer, sliding safely into a base and once again spearheading a Milwaukee Brewers rally. This was Robin Yount, the dirt bike king, making like Knievel on the desert dunes of Yuma, Arizona.

One day the landing didn't come off quite right. Yount, the Brewers' multimillion-dollar star, was dragged 40 feet on his back. His back was a bloody mess.

Then there was the time he was racing a sports car and he took the corner wrong at 120 miles per hour and flipped. He survived without injury but totaled the car.

And what about the day he was competing in a go-kart race and the driver behind him crashed so hard into Yount's car that he went right over his back and landed on top of him. "That sure was funny," said Yount.

So the question is: What's an all-star baseball player doing taking his life in his hands by racing vehicles at high speed?

"Living on the edge is the only way to play—baseball or whatever," said Yount.

Robin R. Yount knew only one way to approach baseball, and life, and that was at full speed. A major league regular at the tender age of 18, he played the game with a high-octane energy and was one of the game's most durable and most athletic players for 20 years (1974-93).

Yount spent his entire major league career with the Milwaukee Brewers and was known for his versatility. He is one of only three players to win Most Valuable Player honors at two positions, capturing the award as a shortstop in 1982 and again as a center fielder in 1989. Stan Musial and Hank Greenberg are the only other players to accomplish that feat, as outfielders and first basemen.

What set Yount apart, however, was his ability to master defensively both positions. He's the only American Leaguer ever to lead the league in fielding percentage as both an infielder and an outfielder.

Yount was the most popular player in Brewers history, leading the team to its only World Series appearance in 1982 and becoming the only player in the team's history to reach the 3,000 hit club. Yount finished with 3,142 hits, including 251 home runs, and he had a lifetime batting average of .285.

Paul Molitor, who played with Yount for 15 seasons, also reached the 3,000 hit club, but his milestone hit came as a member of the Toronto Blue Jays.

Statistics weren't at all important to Yount. "He has never known what his batting average was, no way," said Jim Gantner, a former teammate. "He just cared about the W."

It is a wonder that Yount played as long as he did, considering his penchant for fast cars and motorcycles. He often competed in motocross, go-kart, and auto races and survived several crashes.

Yount believed that concentration was the key to his survival. He was remarkably injury free during the first 10 years of his career. In the demanding position of shortstop, he was able to play more than 140 games a season in eight of those 10 years.

"I can blot things out and tunnel my focus," Yount said. "To me, concentration is the one skill that ties together every sport—golf, baseball, racing. You know how people get hurt on motorcycles or in race cars or in baseball? They don't concentrate."

Born in Danville, Illinois, on September 16, 1966, Robin was the youngest of three sons of Phil Yount, a chemical engineer, and his wife, Marion. At the time of Robin's birth, the family lived in Covington, Indiana, where Robin's father worked for the DuPont Chemical Company. But when Robin was one year old, Phil took a job as an aerospace engineer with Rocketdyne, a division of Rockwell International, and the family moved to Woodland Hills, California. It was in this upper-middle-class suburb of Los Angeles that Yount grew up.

The Younts' ranch-style house in Woodland Hills had a backyard that was 330 feet long and 70 feet wide. It was used as a baseball diamond, football field, golf course, and motorcycle track by Robin and his brothers. Robin learned how to ride a motorcycle at age 11, and when he was 13, he competed in his first motocross race.

"As kids in California, we rode the hills all day," said Yount. "We chased jackrabbits. We did wheelies on mountaintops. In high school I spent all my time on the baseball field and in the machine shop—working on motorcycles."

One of Robin's brothers, Larry, was a standout baseball pitcher in high school and played for several years in the minor leagues. On one occasion, he made it briefly to the major leagues with the Houston Astros.

Larry played for Oklahoma City in Triple A when Robin was at Taft High School. During the summer of his sophomore and junior years, Robin stayed with his brother during homestands. Sometimes Robin would work out with the team.

During Robin's junior year in high school, the family built a batting cage out of chicken wire in the backyard. In the off-seasons, when Larry was home, he'd take Robin to the batting cage or a nearby field and pitch to him.

"Sometimes he'd throw real stuff," recalled Robin. "That was great experience. Here I was, a high school player, swinging at Triple A pitching."

The extra work with Larry paid off. In his senior year, Robin batted .458 and was named the outstanding high school baseball player in Los Angeles. The Brewers selected the 17-year-old Yount third in the June 1973 draft. He turned down a scholarship from Arizona State to sign with Milwaukee.

Milwaukee sent him to its Class A farm club in the New York-Pennsylvania League, where he batted .285 in 64 games. His performance earned him an invitation to spring training in 1974.

Yount caught the eye of Brewers manager Del Crandall in spring training. The Brewers were beginning their sixth season as an expansion team and had never finished higher than next-to-last in their division. Moreover, Milwaukee's starting shortstop in 1973, Tim Johnson, had batted only .213, so Crandall decided to give Yount chance at the position.

Even though he had to sit out the last month of the season with tendinitis in his ankle, Yount's first year with the Brewers was respectable. Playing in 107 games, he hit .250. Yount also was fortunate in that he was able to break into baseball in a small market rather than in the glare of a big-city spotlight. He also benefited from playing with Hank Aaron, baseball's all-time home run king, who was winding down his career in Milwaukee. Aaron taught Yount a lot about batting preparation, including what pitch to look for in a certain situation.

Another major influence on Yount's development as a player was Harvey Kuenn, who was the batting coach when Yount joined the team and who later managed the Brewers. Kuenn, a former batting champion and All-Star shortstop, put in long hours teaching the rudiments of the game to Yount.

In his second year, Yount improved his average to .267 and doubled his RBI total to 52. However, he was abysmal in the field, committing a league-leading 44 errors at shortstop, most of them on throws. In 1976, he reduced his errors to 31 but saw his batting average tumble to .252. He was clearly not developing as quickly as the Brewers anticipated.

As early as 1977, the Brewers' front office discussed the idea of shifting Yount to center field. But they decided to stick with him another year, and he showed vast improvement. Playing in over 145 games for the third consecutive season, Yount again lowered his error total and hit a respectable .288.

But in spring training of 1978, Yount was at a crossroads. Baseball hadn't been as much fun as he thought it would be. The team was bad, and his contract had expired. Moreover, his ankles were hurting from tendinitis, and he was off to a poor start in the exhibition season.

Even worse, Michelle Edelstein, a California girl who had lived with him during the previous season, wasn't sure she wanted to accompany him back to Milwaukee for another season, at least not unless they were married. She was clearly putting him on the spot and refused to come to Arizona for spring training.

As a result, Yount left spring training to contemplate his future. Rumors began circulating that some wealthy men from Palm Springs, California, were going to underwrite him on the pro golf tour. Yount had been playing golf since he was a youngster, and his friends admitted he could be a scratch golfer if he worked at it.

Paul Molitor, a promising youngster, was inserted at shortstop and played well. If Yount did not come back, the Brewers were confident that Molitor could do the job.

Club president Bud Selig and general manager Harry Dalton talked to Yount and were confident they would get him to sign a new contract. The team's new manager, George Bamberger, also talked to him and came away with the same notion. But the season opened and still Yount was unsigned. But not until early May, after he ironed out the problems with his girlfriend and set a wedding date for the next winter, did he sign his contract. After working out with the team, he was reinstated at shortstop, and Molitor was shifted to second. The two men would play together for 15 seasons and form the best one-two punch in club history.

While many teams would have animosity toward a player who bolted the team and then returned, the Brewers welcomed Yount back. They appreciated his hard work and team play, and he responded by hitting .293 and knocking in 71 runs. With the rookie Molitor contributing a .273 average and scoring 78 runs, the Brewers posted a 93-68 record, which was good for third place in the AL East. The following year, Yount slumped to .267, but the team went 95-66 and was establishing itself as a perennial contender.

Yount knew he was going to have to get stronger if he were ever to reach his potential in the major leagues. During the winter of 1978-79, Yount embarked on a weight program. He added significant muscle to his 6-foot frame and the results were remarkable: a .293 batting average plus 23 homers and a league-leading 49 doubles.

Not only was Yount improving at the plate, bit he also was improving in the field. In 1981, a season that was shortened because of a players' strike, Yount committed only six errors in 91 games and led the minors in fielding percentage for shortstops. He had always had great range in the field, but now he was finally harnessing his erratic arm. Yount also hit .273 with 10 homers and 49 RBI in the shortened season, and the Brewers met the New York Yankees for the East Division crown in the special playoff format that was used because of the players' strike. Yount hit .316 against the Yankees in the best-of-five series, but New York won, three games to two.

The Brewers finally put it all together in 1982 and won the AL pennant for the only time in Yount's career. The team, managed by Harvey Kuenn, became known as "Harvey's Wallbangers" because of its power-hitting attack, and Yount led the way. He batted .331 with 29 homers and 114 RBI. He led the major leagues in hits, slugging percentage, and total bases and tied for first in doubles. He was the first AL shortstop ever to lead the league in both total bases and slugging percentage in one season. In addition, he won a Gold Glove for fielding excellence. Not surprisingly, he was named the league's Most Valuable Player.

Yount's crowning moment of the season came on the final day. The Brewers had lost three straight games at Baltimore to fall into a tie for first place with the Orioles. The Orioles had their ace pitcher, Jim Palmer, on the mound going for the clincher. But Yount homered in his first two times at-bat and added a triple later in the game to pace the Brewers to a 10-2 triumph.

In the best-of-five AL Championship Series, the Brewers lost the first two games, then won three in a row to take the title, becoming the first team to rally from an 0-2 deficit and win. The Brewers met the NL-champion St. Louis Cardinals in the World Series, and Yount twice collected four hits in a game and batted .414. But the Cardinals rallied from a 3-2 deficit to win the final two games and claim the championship.

Robin had been an amazingly durable player during his first nine seasons, but in the second half of the 1983 season, he began an injury-plagued period. It started with a herniated disc, which was quickly dissolved by injection. Then came a shoulder injury in 1984 that required arthroscopic surgery. During spring training of 1985, he was moved to left field because he could no longer make the throws from shortstop.

In the middle of the season, the Brewers moved him to center field, but he found it difficult to throw out runners. More surgery was required. This time he felt his career was in jeopardy. He had no desire to be a designated hitter and contemplated retirement if he could no longer make throws from the outfield.

"If the operation didn't work, I would have said, 'It's been nice,' and I would have gone on to other things," he said. "I love baseball, and I wanted to keep playing. But I was prepared to leave it. I didn't see myself as a DH."

The doctors took a more aggressive approach this time, removing bone spurs and calcium deposits, then smoothing out the bone. It worked. By spring training of 1986, he was able to throw out runners from center field. He made only one error in the outfield that season and became the first player in AL history to have led the league in fielding percentage as an infielder and an outfielder.

He was showing no signs of slowing down as a hitter, either. Yount strung together four consecutive .300 seasons at the plate from 1987 to 1989, culminating in another MVP award in 1989. The Brewers finished only .500 that year, but Robin hit .318 with 21 homers, 103 RBI, and 101 runs scored. He narrowly beat out Texas slugger Ruben Sierra for the award.

But individual awards didn't mean much to Robin. The team was the thing, and the Brewers were no longer winning much. He also was unhappy about the selfishness of some of the younger players, who put their personal achievements ahead of the team. He longed to play for a contender again, and so armed with an MVP award, he became a free agent after the 1989 season and began negotiating with several teams. The Angels were very interested, but a massive letter-writing campaign by Milwaukee fans urging Yount to stay convinced the Brewers' star to return.

Yount was nearing the end, however. He played four more seasons with Milwaukee, but hit no higher than .264 in any of those seasons. His one remaining highlight came on September 9, 1992, when he singled off Cleveland relief pitcher Jose Mesa for his 3,000th career hit. A crowd of 47,589 showed up at County Stadium to witness the event, and even the usually placid Yount was caught up in the excitement of the event.

"It's a lot more exciting than I ever have envisioned," Yount said. "I said all along it's not any big deal, not what you play the game for. But the excitement level is turned up a notch."

The 1993 season was Robin's last. The quiet leader of the Brewers for 20 years could no longer handle the physical grind of the long season. Five years after his retirement, he was elected to the Hall of Fame in his first year of eligibility.

Although he left some indelible statistics in the archives of the Brewers, Yount's contributions to the team and the game go far beyond mere numbers.

"I'd like to be known as a person who went out and gave it everything he had every game," Yount said. "I feel I did that as best I could."

Tony Gwynn

Ranking: 18th
Hit Total: 3,141

AP/Wide World Photos

The "habit" began quite innocently. Tony Gwynn and his wife, Alicia, purchased a video camera in 1983, one year after the birth of their son, Anthony, in order to record the child's growth. Many couples do that, then put the camera aside once the child has grown.

But one day during the 1983 season, Gwynn found himself in a batting slump so bad that San Diego manager Dick Williams was forced to bench him. The Padres were on the road and Gwynn was mortified, so he called home and asked his wife to record his next series of at-bats on their VCR.

"Just hit the record button when I come to the plate," he told her.

When Gwynn got home and looked at the tape, he saw right away what he was doing wrong at the plate.

"I couldn't wait to get to the ballpark and correct it. It took me 15 swings. I hit .333 the rest of the year."

Since then, the videotape has become as much a part of his equipment as his bats. A legend has grown around Gwynn and his remote control. Before each game he plays, he hooks up his VCR to the clubhouse monitor. Then, with a second VCR he carries, he will transfer his at-bats to another tape. Next, he will edit those at-bats onto three separate tapes—one for good at-bats, where he might have worked the counts, fouled off tough pitches, and generally not been embarrassed; one for at-bats in which he got hits; and one for the swings that actually produced the hits.

"If there are bad at-bats on the tapes, I just click them out," Gwynn said. "Watch 'em once, click 'em out. You don't want to watch yourself looking like an idiot, waving at some curveball."

Gwynn has refined his system considerably since he first started making tapes of each at-bat. When he first started doing it, he would carry 11 tapes on the road—one for each of the teams in the league. Baseball expansion and *improved technology helped him perfect the procedure. Still, some people find Gwynn's habit irritating.*

"It drives people crazy," he admitted. "It's tedious, splitting cables and everything, and I know it gets on people's nerves. But it works. In this game, if you're successful, that means getting hits three out of 10 times. I'm trying to tap into the other 70 percent, and I don't mind doing it. It's not hard spending 20 minutes a day—pause, record, fast forward."

Oh, yes, this attention Gwynn pays to detail has resulted in eight batting titles—the most in National League history.

Anthony Keith Gwynn demonstrated a work ethic that enabled him to acquire a status as the all-time franchise player in San Diego Padres history. A left-handed slap hitter who also gradually turned himself into one of the National League's best defensive right fielders, Gwynn won batting titles in 1984, 1987, 1988, 1989, 1994, 1995, 1996, and 1997. He also led the NL in hits five times and in runs scored once.

Although often prodded by his father and other confidants to leave the small market of San Diego for greater riches in larger cities, Gwynn has been content to play his entire career away from the big-city lights and in the comfortable obscurity of laid-back Southern California.

Though he might have earned an elusive World Series ring with another team, Gwynn did at least have the opportunity to play in two World Series. The Padres lost to the Detroit Tigers in the 1984 Series and to the New York Yankees in the 1998 Series.

Born in Los Angeles on May 9, 1960, Gwynn moved with his family to Long Beach, California, when he was 8. Gwynn's father, Charles, was a warehouseman for the State of California and his mother, Vendella, a postal employee. On weekends and during the summer, Tony would play all day in his backyard with his older brother, Charles, and younger brother, Chris.

Charles, who Tony considered the best athlete in the family, played college baseball for Cal State-Los Angeles, and Chris played baseball at San Diego State and later made it to the major leagues.

"We stared out playing Wiffle Ball," Tony recalled, "but we'd break them, and my mother and father got tired of buying new ones. We started making balls out of socks, but that got to be expensive, too. We found that we could take big, thick white socks, cut them up, and make maybe five or six balls out of one with rubber bands and tape.

"Our bat was one that a guy was about to put in a trash can at a softball field near our house. It was broken, but we nailed it back together and cut off the end so it wouldn't be so heavy.

"Our backyard was so small that the pitcher would be maybe 15 feet from the batter. You had to be quick with the bat. We got where we could throw sinkers and sliders and curves. We'd play from early in the morning until the sun went down."

As a youngster, Gwynn's best sport was basketball, not baseball. He was such a good point guard at Long Beach Poly High that he was heavily recruited by Texas Christian and San Diego State. He wasn't even selected in the baseball draft, despite hitting .560 as a senior and making the all-city team.

"Baseball was just something to do in the spring and summer," Gwynn said. "I told my mom I didn't think I would try baseball in college. She and my dad told me it was something I might want to fall back on."

Gwynn accepted a scholarship to San Diego State, but he felt out of place there, and considered quitting school. At the end of his freshman year, Aztecs basketball coach Tom Vezie advised him not to play baseball.

"The rest of the school year was miserable," said Gwynn. "I would sit on the right-field fence, watching the baseball team play. It was the first time I had ever really missed it."

At the end of Gwynn's sophomore basketball season, Vezie was fired. "After that, there was nothing to keep me from playing baseball," said Gwynn. "I got to thinking that there probably wasn't a future in the NBA for anyone who is 5-11. I figured I better change my priorities and shoot for a career in baseball."

The Aztecs fielded a strong team in Gwynn's junior year, and a lot of the team's players were drafted. Gwynn wanted to play for the Dodgers, his boyhood favorite, but was surprised and pleased when the Padres took him in the third round.

Gwynn, who had set a San Diego State career assists record in basketball, also learned that the San Diego Clippers had selected him in the 10th round of the National Basketball Association draft.

Figuring his chances of making it professionally were better in baseball, Gwynn signed with the Padres. He was assigned to Walla Walla, Washington, of the Northwest League, and he and his new bride arrived there in the summer of 1981. Gwynn showed right away that he was an accomplished hitter, as he batted .331 in 42 games. Promoted to Amarillo of the Texas League, he hit .462 in 23 games.

Gwynn opened the 1982 season with Hawaii of the Pacific Coast League and hit .328 in 93 games. The Padres called him up later in the season, and Gwynn hit .289 in his first 54 major league games. He ended up missing the last three weeks of the season, however, after breaking his left wrist diving for a ball in Pittsburgh.

An injury to his right wrist four months later sidelined him the first 10 weeks of the 1983 season. However, he came back to hit .309 in 86 games and, aided by those videotapes, finished the season with a 25-game hitting streak in September.

By 1984, he was an All-Star. In his first full major league season, Gwynn led the NL with a .351 batting average and set a club record with 213 hits. He also knocked in 71 runs and, moreover, the Padres won the NL West title, then defeated the Chicago Cubs, three games to two, for the franchise's first NL pennant. Although the Padres lost to Detroit in five games in the World Series, it was assumed the team would be a contender for years to come.

But it would be another 14 years before Gwynn made it back to the World Series.

The years 1984-89 were pivotal ones in the development of Gwynn as a complete major league player. He worked hard at improving his baserunning and defense. During those six years, he became an accomplished base stealer, notching 206 stolen bases in that span, including a high of 56 in 1987.

He also became a top-notch outfielder, winning five Gold Gloves from 1986 to 1991. His strong arm enabled him to reach double figures in assists six times.

Gwynn won three consecutive batting titles from 1987 to 1989, and it was during those years that he realized he was being grossly underpaid by the Padres. He had signed a six-year, $4.6 million contract in 1984, which at the time looked like a good deal. But free agency had sent salaries soaring.

After hitting .350 in 1987, Gwynn went into Padres president Chub Feeney's office and asked for a contract extension. He wanted a two-year extension at $1.6 million per season.

When he heard Gwynn's demands, Feeney began to laugh.

"He laughed so hard, he spit cigar ashes all over my face," said Gwynn. "There are some things you never forget, and I'll never forget that."

Gwynn figured he'd just have to wait until after the 1990 season to get paid what he was worth, but in 1989, Padres president Dick Freeman telephoned Gwynn and offered a two-year extension.

They agreed on a two-year extension for $2 million in 1991 and 1992, including a $200,000 bonus. But one year later, the contract was out-dated. By 1990, Gwynn was the seventh-highest-paid player on the Pa-dres, and about 100 players were making more than he was.

Gwynn's dedication to the Padres and the game of baseball probably cost him another batting title in 1991. Even though hobbled by a sore knee, he was batting .337 late in the season and was seemingly on his way to his fifth batting crown when the knee began hurting badly. His father told Tony to quit for the season.

"You're not helping yourself, you're not helping your team," he said. "Sit down and win your title."

Gwynn, however, played on, and his batting average tumbled to .317. He finally quit for the season to have arthroscopic surgery, and Atlanta's Terry Pendleton emerged as the batting champion.

Gwynn's father was beside himself. "I told you, I told you!" he screamed at Tony.

Tony, however, knew he could never sit out and win a batting title. "Dad, you can't win a batting title that way. You just can't," Tony said.

Gwynn would go on to win three more batting titles, but his father would not be around to see them. He died in 1993. "That fifth title bugged him forever," Gwynn said.

When Gwynn's contract expired after the 1992 season, his father was adamant that Tony leave San Diego. The Padres were backing up the truck at the time and unloaded much of their talent. Gwynn was about the only valuable commodity they had left.

"The team isn't going anywhere," Charles Gwynn told his son. "Get out of Dodge!"

Gwynn, however, refused to leave. He liked the low profile of San Diego, the beautiful weather, and the soft grass and inviting gaps at Jack Murphy Stadium.

"I'm happy here," Tony said. "One of the reasons I've been successful is that I'm not bigger than big. There's not that much pressure, not that much hype here. You've got to have time and room to work at your craft. They aren't that demanding in San Diego."

Early in 1994, only months after his father died of heart problems, Gwynn went to the Padres and told them he would prefer to stay in San Diego rather than become a free agent. The Padres suggested a contract extension, and Tony agreed to a $4 million-a-year contract through 1997, with an option year and some bonuses thrown in.

The 1994 season will forever be remembered as the one in which a strike forced cancellation of the last two months of the season and all of the postseason games. For Gwynn, the strike may have prevented him from batting .400.

He hit .394 in 110 games that season to win his fifth batting title, but the season ended on August 12. Who knows what might have happened had the season played out to the end?

"There was no pressure to that point," said Gwynn. "The pressure would have come in September. I had talked to Rod Carew (.388 in 1977) and George Brett (.390 in 1980), asked what it was like to make a run at .400. Both said it was unbelievable, so tough to go about your business. Now I'm not a Pete Rose, a guy who thrives on that kind of attention. But I kind of wanted to go through it, to get a taste of it. You don't really know what you're made of until you do. I don't think I'd been destroyed by it, but you can't really say, can you?"

A year after flirting with .400, Tony won another batting title by hitting .368. In some ways, though, it was his most satisfying season, since he also drove in 90 runs. It marked the first time he had driven in more than 72 runs in a season.

Tony only got into 116 games because of an injured Achilles tendon in 1996, but he managed to win a third straight batting title by hitting .353. He had shown he was still a solid hitter, yet some baseball people were beginning to question his status as an everyday player. The Achilles tendon had required surgery, and his once-lean frame was now supporting considerable girth.

But Gwynn went on a rigid rehabilitation program. He shot 100 jump shots a day, ran up and down the escalators at Jack Murphy Stadium, and sprinted with a parachute rigged to his back. As a result, his legs were stronger than they'd been in five years.

Gwynn also took to heart a conversation he had with Ted Williams before the start of the 1996 season. Williams, the last player to hit .400, told Gwynn he should be hitting the inside pitch for power instead of being content to hit it the opposite way for a single. But a heel injury suffered in the 13th game of the season prevented Gwynn from ever applying that advice during the season. He could not plant firmly enough on that foot to take an aggressive swing at the ball. As a result, despite his .353 average, he collected only three homers and 50 RBI.

As he entered the 1997 campaign, however, he decided to try to implement what Williams had told him. The results were remarkable. At the age of 37, Gwynn enjoyed the best season of his career, batting .372 with 220 hits, including career highs in home runs (17) and RBI (119).

He enjoyed the 1998 season even more, however, as the Padres reached the World Series for only the second time in his career. Limited to 127 games because of injuries, Tony hit .321 during the regular season as the Padres won the NL West. The fact that they eventually were swept by the Yankees in the World Series diminished only slightly Gwynn's satisfaction from the season.

Entering the 1999 season, Gwynn needed just 72 hits to join the 3,000 hit club. He achieved his goal on August 6 with a single off Montreal rookie Dan Smith in the first inning. Even though the game was being played in Montreal's Olympic Stadium, the Expos' management set off fireworks in honor of the historic hit. It was the first of four hits in the game for Gwynn, who became the first NL player in 20 years to reach the 3,000 hit plateau.

Gwynn finished the 1999 season with 3,067 hits and could finish among the top 10 in career hits before he retires. He is a certain first-ballot Hall of Fame electee, once he becomes eligible.

Editor's note:
At the time of the first publication of this volume, Tony Gwynn was at the top of his game. He has since retired and transitioned from powerhouse athlete to living legend. "Mr. Padre" took off his uniform for the last time in 2001, after 20 years on the field. He retired with a .338 batting average and appeared as an All-Star 15 times (10 appearances occurred consecutively from 1989-1999). He was elected to the Baseball Hall of Fame in 2007.

Dave Winfield

Ranking: 19th
Hit Total: 3,110

AP/Wide World Photos

He had borne the weight of postseason failure for more than a decade, and now Dave Winfield had a chance to rid himself of that one blemish on an otherwise outstanding major league career.

It was the 11th inning of Game 6 of the 1992 World Series, and the Toronto Blue Jays had the winning run on second base as Winfield stood in the batter's box facing the Atlanta Braves pitcher, Charlie Leibrandt.

Only three weeks earlier, Winfield turned 41, and the clock was running down on a career that had begun in another time zone some 18 years back. He needed to make good on this at-bat, needed to show everyone that he was indeed a "winner" and not a player who would leave baseball with gaudy statistics, but also with a tag that said, "Can't win the big ones."

It was an albatross that had hung over Winfield for his failure to lead the New York Yankees to a World Series title in his nine seasons with them as one of the game's brightest stars in the world's biggest showcase.

He was practically assured of a place in the Hall of Fame, but it would never be enough for him unless he could prove once and for all that he could be counted on to come through in the clutch. During his previous 18 big-league seasons, he had made it to the World Series only once, and it was a time he wanted to forget. Except, of course, no one ever let him.

The previous World Series trip came in 1981, Winfield's first year in New York, when the Yankees lost to the Los Angeles Dodgers in six games. Winfield, who led the team in hits, total bases, and game-winning RBI during the strike-shortened regular season, was horrible in the World Series, going 1-for-22.

Winfield had several outstanding seasons with the Yankees after that, but the team never made it back to the postseason. Winfield was the biggest name *with the biggest contract, so fans put much of the blame on him. Outspoken owner George Steinbrenner had even gone so far as to label Winfield "Mr. May," in mock contrast to the "Mr. October" tag that had been hung on another Yankee slugger, Reggie Jackson, for his consistent postseason heroics.*

Winfield and Steinbrenner would have an antagonistic relationship for most of his years with the Yankees.

But now he was with Toronto, and he stood at the plate with two out and two runners on base in the top of the 11th inning with the scored tied, 2-2. In the stands, his mother-in-law was praying for Winfield to deliver and exorcise the demons. Leibrandt worked the count to 3-2, then delivered a change-up. Had it been a fastball, Winfield's aging reflexes might not have caught up with it. But he got around on this pitch and hit it down the left-field line for a double that scored two runs and put the Blue Jays ahead, 4-2.

Atlanta would come back to score a run in the bottom of the inning, but the Blue Jays held on to win, 4-3, and bring Canada its first baseball world championship. Winfield had finally cut loose the albatross.

David Mark Winfield was an athletic marvel. He was drafted for three professional sports—football, baseball, and basketball—out of the University of Minnesota and could have played any of them well. He chose baseball and played 22 years in the major leagues, completing his final season when he was 45 years old. He had 3,110 hits, including 465 homers, and is one of only seven players in baseball history to collect at least 3,000 hits and 400 homers.

A 6-foot-6, 220-pound outfielder, Winfield was a run-producer of the first order. He knocked in 100 or more runs in a season eight times, including five years in a row (1982-86). He scored 90 or more runs in a season eight times, .300 or better four times, and hit 20 or more homers in a season 14 times. His 1,107 RBI in the decade from 1979 to 1988 were more than any other major league hitter. Yet he never led the league in any major offensive category.

Winfield also was a stellar defensive player. A right fielder for most of his career, he won seven Gold Gloves. He had a strong arm and won notoriety with it when he killed a seagull with a warm-up throw between innings of a 1983 contest in Toronto. The seagull is a protected species in Canada, and the incident nearly resulted in prosecution after some claimed that Winfield had deliberately taken aim at the bird.

A soft-spoken, articulate man, Winfield was almost as well known for his charity work, most notably the David M. Winfield Foundation, a trust set up to fund youth programs. It was Winfield's insistence that part of his salary with the Yankees be given to the foundation that was at the center of his feud with Steinbrenner.

Winfield came into this world on a very historic baseball day. He was born in St. Paul, Minnesota, on October 3, 1951—the day Bobby Thomson hit the dramatic home run for the New York Giants that beat the Brooklyn Dodgers for the National League pennant.

Three years after he was born, his father, Frank Winfield, a dining-car waiter on the Great Northern Railroad, and his wife, Arline, separated. From that time on, David and his older brother, Steve, were raised by their mother and grandmother. It would take many years before Winfield was able to establish a relationship with his father.

"Considering that we grew up in a broken home, we had a happy childhood," Winfield recalled.

One of the reasons was Bill Peterson, the director of the Oxford Playground, which was only a half a block away from the Winfield home. Peterson was a white man who lived in a black community. He was a coach, surrogate father, and friend to Winfield and his brother during their youth.

The Winfield brothers learned how to play basketball and baseball at the Oxford Playground, but baseball was their favorite sport. Dave did not try out for baseball until his junior year—after he'd grown five inches in one year—and he didn't make an impression on anyone in basketball until his senior year.

In his senior year of high school, he made all-city and all-state in both sports. He was a pitcher in baseball, and the Boston Red Sox wanted to sign him. But after talking it over with his mother and brother, he decided against signing with the Red Sox because he was wary about how black players were treated in the minor leagues.

Instead, he accepted a college scholarship to the University of Minnesota, but during the summer of his freshman year, he got into trouble with the law. He was arrested as an accomplice in the theft of a snowblower from a Minneapolis hardware store.

"My mother came to the jail and there were tears in her eyes," Winfield remembered. "I pledged to my mother that I would never do anything like that again, ever. I was lucky. They let me go. But I was on probation the rest of my time in college."

The incident helped Winfield turn his life around. He began paying attention to his studies and maintained a B average over the next three years and left college just a few credits short of his degree.

He made the varsity baseball team in his sophomore year and won eight of 11 starts. However, he hurt his arm in his junior year and finished the season alternating between first base and left field. In his senior year, he returned part-time to the mound and posted a 13-1 record and struck out 109. He also hit .385 with nine home runs and 33 RBI. He was named to the college All-America team and earned Most Valuable Player honors in the NCAA Tournament.

In basketball, he jumped from an intramural team to the varsity in his junior year. When starting power forward Ron Behagen got hurt, Winfield replaced him and averaged 11 points and six rebounds per game in the final 11 games. Minnesota finished 21-4 to win the Big Ten Conference title.

When Behagen returned the following year, Winfield went back to the bench; but when he did play, he rebounded well and played solid defense.

In 1973, Winfield was drafted by four teams in three sports. The San Diego Padres selected him in baseball, the Atlanta Hawks of the NBA and the Utah Stars of the ABA chose him in basketball, and the Minnesota Vikings of the NFL took him in football, even though Winfield had never played football in high school or college. The Vikings thought his size and speed would make him a good receiver.

"Football was out of the question," Winfield recalled. "It just wasn't my game. I contemplated pro basketball, but from the time I was a little boy and people asked me what I wanted to be, I always said a professional baseball player."

Winfield elected to go with the Padres and received an $18,000 salary and a $50,000 bonus. Although he had always been primarily a pitcher in high school and college, the Padres saw him as an everyday player. In fact, they did not even bother sending him to the minors.

"Two days after I signed, I was in a uniform in center field," he said. "Those first months in San Diego were the hardest of my life. I was seeing pitches I'd never seen before. I was playing in a ballpark the size of an airport. I'd get my legs all tangled up in the outfield. I was holding my hands too low on the bat. I was hitching my swing, overstriding, overswinging. I'd been a pitcher. Now I was an outfielder. I was thrown into a sink-or-swim situation. I learned to swim the hard way."

Since the Padres were not a pennant contender, they could let Winfield learn at his own pace. He worked hard at becoming more than a power hitter and batted over .300 (.308) for the first time in 1978. He became one of the best line-drive hitters in baseball, but after five years with the Padres, he was beginning to get tired of the losing and longed for a place to play where his talents could be showcased.

"There aren't 10 better players than me in the National League," Winfield claimed during the 1977 season. "People always want to know why Winfield is not winning ball games. Well, one man, two men, three men can't do it . . . If the Padres go places, I will be a main reason, but if they falter, I'll still shine."

Meanwhile, Winfield had forged a friendship with a man named Albert S. Frohman, a former big-band pianist and kosher food caterer from Brooklyn. Frohman became Winfield's agent and negotiated several pay raises in San Diego. But Frohman was convinced that Winfield would never flourish in a losing environment like San Diego and convinced his client that he should move on. Since free agency came into effect in 1976, several players had sold themselves to the highest bidder, and clubs were willing to pay top dollar for players of Winfield's caliber.

Winfield trusted Frohman implicitly and followed his advice. The team that intrigued Winfield the most was the Yankees. There were four reasons: Steinbrenner was known to spend lavishly for big-name talent, the Yankees were perennial pennant contenders, New York was a city that could offer him a future in business after baseball, and it was a city where his programs for underprivileged children would flourish.

Steinbrenner's scouts told him that Winfield had the talent to put the Yankees on top again. It was agreed that the Yankees would try and sign the outfielder after he became a free agent following the 1980 season. The Yankees outbid the other interested teams and signed Winfield to a 10-year pact worth $23,906,134, with cost-of-living increases. He also received a signing bonus of $1 million, bringing the contract to a then-record $25 million. It was agreed that half of each year's cost-of-living increase would be contributed to the David M. Winfield Foundation.

Baseball management throughout the league was aghast at the size of the contract.

"I don't think any athlete in any team sport can be important enough to command that kind of money," said Hank Peters, the Baltimore Orioles' general manager. "

But Winfield had a quick retort for his detractors: "Everything has a market value. How do you set a price on a precious gem?" he said.

Winfield had a solid first season with the Yankees, even though the campaign was shortened by the strike and resulted in a bizarre split season. But he hit only .154 in the Yankees' victory over the Oakland A's in the American League Championship Series and then .045 in the World Series loss to the Dodgers. When Winfield finally got a hit late in the Series, he asked for the ball as a keepsake, a decision that angered Steinbrenner.

A year later, trouble between Winfield and Steinbrenner began to escalate. It started initially when Steinbrenner refused to pay half of Winfield's cost-of-living increases into the Winfield Foundation, as agreed upon in Winfield's contract. Steinbrenner said he was made aware of "financial irregularities" in the foundation and would not pay until those were straightened out. However, the foundation filed a suit against Steinbrenner, and the two parties settled out of court for more than $100,000.

The seeds of discontent had been planted. During the summer of 1982, Steinbrenner publicly stated that Winfield wasn't a winner and couldn't carry a club the way Reggie Jackson could. A year later, the Winfield Foundation filed another suit against Steinbrenner for non payment. Once again, there was an out-of-court settlement, this time more than $300,000.

The rancor between the two continued for the rest of Winfield's stay with the Yankees, culminating in Steinbrenner's paying $40,000 to Howard Spira, a former professional gambler and one-time employee of the foundation, for information damaging to Winfield. Spira had at first gone to Winfield with a similar offer, but Winfield had refused. When the matter was brought to the attention of baseball commissioner Fay Vincent, Steinbrenner, fearing a long suspension, worked out a deal and removed himself from club affairs. He was back, however, in under three years.

Before the Steinbrenner-Spira connection became public, Winfield was traded to the California Angels. He had missed the entire 1989 season with a back injury and was off to a slow start in 1990. He managed to hit .275 with 19 homers and 72 RBI for the Angels and did even better the following year by hitting 28 homers and knocking in 86 runs.

After the 1991 campaign, the Angels bought out Winfield's contract and he became a free agent again. This time he joined the Blue Jays, who were looking for a veteran player to help bring them an elusive pennant. Winfield proved to be a good fit. His manager at Toronto was Cito Gaston, a former teammate of Winfield's in San Diego. Placed in the cleanup slot,

Winfield responded with 26 homers and 108 RBI as he led the Blue Jays to the AL East title. They defeated the Oakland A's to win the pennant, then downed the Braves in the World Series. It was Winfield's only season with the Blue Jays.

Winfield went back home to Minnesota in 1993 and signed with the Twins. On September 16, 1993, he reached the 3,000 hit milestone with a single off Oakland relief pitcher Dennis Eckersley. Winfield finished the season with 21 homers and 76 RBI for the Twins, then played one more season with them before finishing his career in 1995 with the Cleveland Indians.

An astute businessman who would often carry a briefcase to the ballpark, Winfield kept busy with his many enterprises following his playing days. As a player, he brought a well-rounded game and an ability to help his team in different ways.

"I think I've offered a lot of intangibles," Winfield said in summing up his career. "I tried to play the whole game. I'm proud I've been able to play the full game. A lot of guys come in and just want to be hitters."

Derek Jeter

Ranking: 20th
Hit Total: 3,088

J *eter is a six-tool player. I've never eaten with him so I can't tell you if he has good table manners, but I would imagine he has those too.*

—The late Johnny Oates, former manager of the Rangers and Orioles

If you were to invent the perfect New York Yankee for the modern era, would you consider a bi-racial shortstop with 3,000 hits who has never been accused of taking steroids? Add on five World Series rings, and you've got the icing on the cake.

For our purposes, Jeter's story begins in 1992 at age eighteen, when the Yankees made him their first-round pick out of Central High in Kalamazoo, Michigan. By May 1995, the well-possessed young man reached the majors for a brief cup of coffee and was the starting shortstop for the most famous baseball team in the world—in 1996 at age 22.

At no point did Jeter appear overawed by his standing. He was celebrated from the beginning for knowing how to play the game right, and almost immediately became a consummate Yankee. His parents raised him right, and he knew how to handle the attention. Teammates appreciated his bravery on the field and opponents appreciated that he never showed them up. The media liked him because he gave good quote; the fans loved him for his effort and results.

While he was a good defensive shortstop, his best tool has always been hitting. From the start of his career, Jeter could line pitches to all fields. He took a lot of pitches and was not afraid of hitting from behind in the count. He struck out a lot, but also drew his share of walks, and hit .291 or better in all but one season through 2011.

As a leadoff man, Jeter topped the AL four times in at-bats, but only once in hits—largely because he walked as often as 91 times in a year.

He was a good base stealer, developed significant power as he went on, and played every day. The Yankees could not have asked for much more.

There have been criticisms of Jeter and his play. He is universally regarded as a shortstop that no longer has the range for the position, and as far as "counting stats," he led the AL in runs once and hits once, and nothing else.

But the writers have liked Jeter; they voted him Rookie of the Year in 1996 and awarded him second in MVP voting in 2006 and third in 1998 and 2009. Jeter also finished in the top ten in MVP voting on three other occasions.

And then there are his World Series rings from 1996, 1998, 1999, 2000, and 2006 . . . and two more AL championships . . . and his .307 batting average and 20 home runs in 152 career post-season games . . . and 12 All-Star games . . . and 3,088 hits.

And there was "the play."

It was the third game of the ALDS on October 13, 2001. The Athletics had defeated the Yankees in the first two games—at Yankee Stadium. Now, in Oakland, the A's could finish things off.

New York led 1–0 in the bottom of the seventh and the home team had Jeremy Giambi on first with two out. Terence Long drilled a liner into the right field corner. As Giambi steamed around the bases with the tying run, with nearly 56,000 fans screaming, Shane Spencer tracked the ball down and uncorked a wild throw toward the plate.

As Giambi lumbered down the third base line toward home, the throw bounced in. Suddenly out of nowhere appeared Jeter, who in one motion grabbed the throw and flipped it to catcher Jorge Posada, who tagged Giambi just before he crossed the plate.

The play changed the entire series. The Yankees won the game, then went on to take the next two, then beat the Seattle Mariners in a five-game ALCS before losing a heartbreaking seven-game series to Arizona. Jeter's amazing reaction play is still celebrated as one of the great moments in Yankees (and postseason) history.

While Jeter's career has begun to wind down, 2011 was a comeback season of sorts following a tough 2010. At thirty-seven, he raised his average 27 points to .297 and collected his 3,000th hit on July 9. Amazingly enough, nobody had ever done this in a Yankee suit, and Jeter did it first, in front of the home folks and second, by putting the ball over the fence.

He took Tampa Bay's young stud David Price yard in the third inning for the magic hit, setting off a huge celebration. But he didn't stop there; Jeter went 5-for-5 on the day, delivering a game-winning single in the eighth.

Signed through 2013 for approximately $17 million a season, Jeter may have to spend more of his time at DH or even third base in the upcoming years. But it wouldn't seem like the Yankees without him in the lineup somewhere.

Jeter rarely had a season that stuck out because it was especially great. But what he has had are 15 seasons remarkable for their quality and consistency. And while there is room in the Hall of Fame for the guys who hit 61 homers in a year or bat .406, there is also room for the consistently excellent who contribute to the best teams of all time.

Craig Biggio

Ranking: 21st
Hit Total: 3,060

I*n some ways, Craig Biggio was a victim of the time in which he played. A seven-time All-Star in the 1990s, he would have been even more celebrated in the 2000s, once Moneyball helped raise the profile of players with high on-base percentage. Biggio made "just" $7 million or so in his prime years, less than a star of comparable results would be making in 2012.*

But after reaching 3,000 hits in 2007, realizing that he was no longer the player he had been and wanting to watch his three kids grow up, he waved goodbye to the game. "I couldn't look my family in the eyes anymore and justify it," Biggio told The New York Times. "It was time to go."

Scrawny rookie catcher Craig Biggio collected his first major league hit on June 29, 1988, against Orel Hershiser of the Dodgers, then perhaps the game's biggest pitching star. But that wasn't enough for the twenty-two-year-old Biggio, who did something that would perfectly express the determination and stick-to-it-iveness that marked his nineteen-year career: he immediately stole second base.

After a star career at Seton Hall, Craig Alan Biggio became the Houston Astros first-round draft pick in 1987.

The young catcher shot quickly through the Houston Astros chain. After hitting .375 in the Class A Sally League in 1987, Biggio leapt to Triple-A Tucson in 1988, batted .320 in 77 games, and earned a promotion to Houston in late June after starter Alan Ashby suffered a back injury.

Trained as a catcher, he displayed the necessary grit and feel for the game to progress through the system at the position.

Once he made the majors, Biggio began to impress with his above-average wheels, strike zone judgment, smart running, and situational hitting. In 1989, his first full season, Biggio batted .264 with 13 home runs and won the Silver Slugger trophy.

He made his first All-Star team in 1991. But the Astros wanted their young project far away from plate collisions, foul tips, and other unwanted results of donning the tools of ignorance...so at age twenty-six, in 1992, Biggio moved to second base full time. He had already played some outfield and second base in 1990 and 1991.

Such a move was nearly unprecedented in baseball history. Not since Ron Brand in the 1960s had a catcher shown significant middle-infield skills, and nobody could think of an All-Star receiver who had moved to the middle infield.

But then, Biggio was always unusual. He didn't have a quick bat, but his eyes were superb, allowing him to follow pitches into the catcher's mitt and slap them to all fields. He wasn't overwhelmingly fast, but knew how to read pitchers and had a good first step.

In the field, he didn't have great hands or a strong arm, but positioned himself well and worked to improve as a fielder. Biggio constantly improved himself, showed energy at all times, gave everything he had on the field, and more than anything else, was a consummate competitor.

Biggio was a hard worker who did lots of little things well. He wasn't a natural infielder, but he learned to play second base. He ran often and intelligently (once leading the NL in steals), developed his batting eye, stretched singles into doubles, and eventually developed the ability to take fat pitches over the wall.

While Biggio never led the league in hits, twice he led in runs because he'd hit around .290 in his peak seasons—take 80 or so walks—and got his body in the way of a lot of pitches (he led the NL five times and still ranks second on the all-time list). He took every edge. He was exceedingly durable, five times leading the NL in plate appearances and three times playing 162 games in a season. Three times he led in doubles.

He was somewhat underrated because: first, he played in Houston and second, he played his entire career in next to slugging first baseman Jeff Bagwell. But Biggio did make seven All-Star teams and in 1997 and 1998 finished fourth and fifth in league MVP voting. He was, of course, beloved in Houston.

Before winning the NL Central in 1997, 1998, and 1999, the Astros hadn't made the post-season since 1986. Biggio, Bagwell, and Derek Bell (later joined by Sean Berry and Lance Berkman) comprised the dangerous "Killer B's," whose power bats propelled the club to the post-season.

Houston won their division again in 2001, but in 1997–99 they went out in the first round of the playoffs. It wasn't until 2004 (when the Astros lost 4–3 in the NLCS) and 2005 (where they fell to the White Sox in the World Series) that Biggio got to play on the game's biggest stages.

While Biggio was never the best player in the game, he was very, very good for several years in the early and mid-1990s. In his mid-30s, however, he began to slow down, and a serious knee injury in 2000 ended his season on August 1.

Biggio came back the next season, and in 2003 volunteered to move to center field, at age thirty-six, to help the team. He returned to second base and ended his career in 2007.

The hard work and all-out hustle took its toll. As he aged, he lost just-thatmuch vision and wrist speed and had to commit earlier on pitches and therefore began walking less frequently, which reduced his offensive value, especially as a leadoff man. But he kept on piling up the base knocks, and entered the action on June 28, 2007, with 2,997 hits.

After grounding out to start the first, Biggio singled in the center and the third off Colorado starter Aaron Cook, bringing him within one of the hallowed 3,000 total.

In the seventh, with Cook still on the mound for the Rockies, Houston trailed 1–0. As more than 42,000 fans cheered, Biggio strode to the plate with two outs and Brad Ausmus, the tying run, on second. Cook worked carefully, and with a 2–0 count, Biggio lined an RBI single to center for his 3,000th big-league base hit. Ausmus scored and the crowd went crazy.

Perhaps carried away with the emotion of the moment, Biggio tried to stretch the hit into a double and was thrown out to end the inning. But in doing so he guaranteed that the Rockies wouldn't make a play at home on Ausmus.

Biggio went on to collect two more hits, going 5-for-6 overall in an 11-inning win. With the Astros down 5–4 in the last of the 11th and two out, Biggio scratched out an infield hit to begin a rally that culminated with Carlos Lee's grand-slam homer.

It was one of Biggio's best individual games, and one of the more exciting contests played by the 73–89 club. Biggio retired following the season with 3,060 hits, having quietly far surpassed expectations that most baseball people had for him and showing through his efforts that hard work, study, and doing the "little things" can make a very big difference indeed.

Rickey Henderson

Ranking: 22nd
Hit Total: 3,055

The only thing I wish I could figure out is how I got misunderstood regarding the type of person I really am and what I accomplished . . . Just because I believed in what I was doing on the field and dedicated myself to playing the game, does that mean I'm cocky? Does that mean I'm arrogant? People who played against me called me cocky, but my teammates didn't. I brought attention, fear.

Born Rickey Nelson Hedley in Chicago on Christmas Day 1958, Henderson eventually took the name of his stepfather.

He was Oakland's fourth-round draft choice out of high school in 1976. In his first full pro season the following year, the youngster swiped 95 bases in the Class A California League. You might say he was in a hurry.

A prototypical leadoff man, Henderson manned the number one spot in the lineup from his very first day in the majors. He debuted with the A's June 24, 1979, and hit .274 at age twenty, swiping 33 bases to rank seventh in the AL despite playing just 89 games.

Henderson entered the AL at a time where speed was at a premium, as Western division teams like Kansas City, Texas, and the Athletics had made base-stealing and forcing opponents' mistakes part of their games.

But Rickey took the approach to a higher level. In 1980, just his second year of big-league ball, he became perhaps the league's dominant offensive player with his combination of on-base ability, foot speed, and running smarts. He made his first of ten All-Star teams and the Athletics, under Billy Martin, improved 29 games to 83–79.

The tough, free-wheeling Martin was just the right manager for a young, aggressive player like Henderson. He gave Henderson the green light to run and in 1980 Henderson went 100 out of 126 in steal attempts, leading the league for the first of seven straight seasons.

Henderson had to a lot of things right to have that many chances to run. Crouching in his stance to create a tiny strike zone, he slapped singles all over the park, chipped in some long hits, and starting in 1980, finished in the top three in on-base percentage five straight seasons.

Only in the strike year of 1981 did he lead the league in hits—he was generally too busy walking 90–100 times a year to do that—but Henderson lasted so long, and was so good, that he got 3,055 safeties anyway.

In 1982, Henderson brought his game a notch higher. While he batted just .267 he slugged ten homers, walked a league-best 116 times, and stole an all-time record 130 bases, literally obliterating the previous record of 118 held by Lou Brock. Nobody has come close to matching Henderson's otherworldly total.

Henderson was the best leadoff man in the history of baseball. He redefined the position to include not only singles hitting and running speed, but all-out aggressiveness on the field, excellent strike-zone judgment, and even power hitting. Five times he led the league in runs.

The perception early on was that Henderson had a weak arm and that you could run on him. In 1981, he threw out 17 runners and won a Gold Glove for his efforts. He was never comfortable in center, but excellent in left.

Such a talent would inevitably be too big for the relatively small Bay Area market, so the New York Yankees acquired Henderson prior to the 1985 season. At age twenty-six, in his first year with a truly good offense around him, Henderson led the AL by scoring 146 runs, hitting .314 with 24 homers and 99 walks, and chipping in a league-best 80 steals to finish third in the league in MVP voting. Despite not winning the trophy, many observers felt that at this time Henderson was the best player in baseball.

This was his peak, but as Henderson aged and he lost some of his speed, he remained productive. He was a good defensive outfielder and developed enough power to set a record for leading off a game with a home run: he did it a rather amazing 81 times.

In 1990, he won the AL's MVP award, hitting .325 and topping the AL in runs and swipes for an Oakland club which advanced to the World Series.

As Henderson edged toward Lou Brock's all-time steals record of 938, he and Brock—the two were friendly—collaborated on a speech. When Henderson smashed the record on May 1, 1991, he was unrepentant in his joy and feeling of validation.

Some felt his head was far too big, and the fact is that Henderson continued to journey throughout his career—in his last 11 seasons he played for eight teams. Perhaps his insistence on the best contract forced his traveling ways; perhaps it was his sometimes prickly personality.

But Henderson gave what he had on the field and remained a productive, often spectacular, offensive player from his first day in the majors to his last. He won two World Series rings and was in the postseason several other times.

During the 2001 season, with San Diego, he claimed all-time marks in walks, runs, and games in left field, and on October 7, the season's last day notched his 3,000th hit, a two-bagger to right against Colorado's John Thomson. Henderson came around to score on another hit and then left the game.

Henderson became known for his unrelenting will to win and also for his unrelenting desire to be paid what he felt he was worth. One of the first players to request—some might say demand—contract renegotiation, he began a nomadic phase of his career in the mid 90s: back to Oakland to Toronto to Oakland again to San Diego and Anaheim, Oakland for a fourth time, the Mets, Seattle, the Padres again, Boston, and, finally, the Dodgers, where in 2003 he played his last big-league game.

Unfortunately, he wanted to continue playing far past the point at which anyone wanted to give him a job. He told the New Yorker, "People always ask me why I still want to play, but I want to know why no one will give me an opportunity. It's like they put a stamp on me: 'Hall of Fame. You're done. That's it.' It's a goddamn shame."

So Henderson went back to the minors, playing in independent leagues, waiting for a call that never came. In 2008, however, he was voted into the Baseball Hall of Fame, and gave a humble and grateful speech.

Henderson has stolen more bases and scored more runs than anyone in baseball history. He ranks second in walks and 22nd in hits. But he was no punch hitter—Henderson ranks 39th all-time in total bases. "The Man of Steal" found more ways to beat you on a baseball field than almost anyone else.

Rod Carew

Ranking: 23rd
Hit Total: 3,053

AP/Wide World Photos

Three hours before the start of a baseball game between the California Angels and the Minnesota Twins, Anaheim Stadium was deserted, except for two lone figures in the infield. One was Angels coach Bobby Knoop, and the other, holding a bat in his hands, was Rod Carew, a seven-time American League batting champion.

They were there long before the arrival of the rest of their team, because Carew, a hitter who had flourished because of his ability to hit the ball to all fields, had suddenly developed a bad habit of pulling every pitch to right field. He hadn't played—except for one pinch-hitting appearance—in a week because of a knee injury, and he was worried about losing the touch that had made him famous.

Here was an artist at work on his canvas trying to recapture an old brush stroke that would turn a mere painting into a masterpiece. For a while it appeared hopeless. Every pitch that Knoop threw, Carew would pull to right field. Finally, Knoop offered some advice.

"Rodney, it looks like you're breaking your wrist too soon," Knoop said. "You're breaking it right at the plate, instead of afterward."

Carew nodded, then went back to work. He took Knoop's advice to heart, and soon he was spraying hits to all parts of the field. Carew had gone from being Andy Warhol to Pablo Picasso again.

Rodney Cline Carew was one of the most disciplined hitters in baseball history. In 19 major league seasons (1967-85) with the Minnesota Twins and California Angels, he compiled a .328 batting average and collected 3,053 hits, including 200 or more in a season four times. He batted .300 or higher for 15 consecutive seasons and was named to the American League All-Star team 18 times. In 1967, he was the AL's Rookie of the Year, and 10 years later, he was named the league's Most Valuable Player.

"Rod was born with great hand-eye coordination, but he worked his rear end off to become a great hitter," said Gene Mauch, who managed Carew for five seasons. "He has 3,000 hits, and he's gotten 100 in practice for every one of those because he's practiced more than anyone you ever saw."

An exceptionally reserved man who disliked the trappings of fame, Carew toiled for most of his career in the relative obscurity of Minnesota. He played for the Twins from 1967 to 1978, before being traded to the California Angels when Twins' owner Calvin Griffith could no longer afford to pay him.

Although his teams never made it to the World Series, Carew played on two AL West championship teams with Minnesota and two more with California. He won batting crowns in 1969, 1972, 1973, 1974, 1975, 1977, and 1978. Carew also excelled in another of the game's artistic skills—the steal of home. He tied the major league record by stealing home seven times in 1969 and accomplished the feat 17 times in his career.

Carew was born on October 1, 1945, on a train that was bound from Gatun, on the Atlantic side of the Panama Canal zone, to Gamboa, Panama, which had a clinic. Rod was delivered by a nurse and a physician, Dr. Rodney Cline, both of whom happened to be passengers on the train. The nurse, Margaret Allen, became the child's godmother, and Rod's mother, Olga Carew, was so thankful to the doctor that she gave Rod the middle name of Cline in the doctor's honor.

One of five children born to Olga and Eric Carew, Rod showed a talent for batting when he was seven. He learned to hit with a broomstick and a tennis ball, but soon came under the tutelage of his uncle, Joseph French, a physical education instructor.

"I always had a talent for baseball," Rod recalled. "I was a superstar at 11. I used to play with boys much older than me. But even then I could hit. I have always been able to hit."

But he also was prone to illness. Carew was sick a lot as a youngster. He contracted rheumatic fever when he was 14 and was hospitalized for six months. When he returned home, his father, a tough, hardworking painter who had labored on the Panama Canal, couldn't believe Rod had been ill. He called him a "sissy" and began to distance himself from his son.

"I never felt close to my dad," Carew recalled. "I was very sick as a kid. There was always something wrong with me. I was timid and quiet. All that time I was in the hospital, my dad never came to see me. I don't know why. I was always very close to my mother."

As a result of his father's indifference, French became a kind of foster father. He took Rod to ball games and encouraged him to pursue his baseball talent.

At the age of 15, the Carew family moved to New York City and lived with Olga's younger brother, Clyde Scott. Scott was a major influence on young Rod, teaching him the importance of family. Rod entered Manhattan's George Washington High School, but as a stranger in a new land and with only limited English skills, he had trouble adjusting to his new country.

"We didn't have any friends," Carew recalled. "The relatives all did everything together. I couldn't go back to my old neighborhoods and say to anybody, 'Hey, I know you.' I went to school and came home. I didn't get involved. Nobody on the block knew us. But, then, I was always a loner, even in Panama."

Although he was getting better at baseball, he had no time to play for the high school team. Afternoons were reserved for part-time work in a drugstore and a grocery store to help the family pay the bills.

He did manage to find time on weekends to play baseball in sandlot games at Macombs Dam Park, adjacent to Yankee Stadium. Within a few weeks, he caught the eye of a "bird dog"—an unofficial unpaid scout—for the Twins. An official scout soon showed up then the Twins' farm director took a look at this spindly youngster with the sweet swing.

Finally, when the Twins came to town to play the Yankees, Minnesota manager Sam Mele summoned Carew to a tryout in Yankee Stadium. Carew, then a skinny 6-foot, 170-pounder, so impressed Mele with his hitting that he was ordered out of the batting cage for fear some Yankee scout might see him.

A month later, the Twins signed Carew for a $5,000 bonus. Less than three years later, he was in the major leagues and starting at second base for the Twins.

Carew had a solid first season, batting .292 in 137 games to earn AL Rookie of the Year honors. He slumped to .273 in 1968, but a year later, he hit .332 and tied the major league record by stealing home seven times.

In 1969, Rod won his first batting title with a .366 average, and the Twins won the American League East pennant. However, they were defeated by the Baltimore Orioles in three straight games in the AL Championship Series.

That year was difficult for Rod on a personal level. His parents separated, and Carew had a hard time dealing with a split in the family, even though he had not had a good relationship with his father.

Billy Martin, then the manager of the Twins, was instrumental in guiding Carew through this difficult period.

"He was like a second father to me," Carew remembered. "I was young back then. I was quiet. People thought I was moody. Billy tried to get me to joke more with the guys, to take things less seriously."

By 1970, however, Martin was gone, and Carew got injured. He tore knee cartilage when a runner barreled into him at second base.

When he returned, he found he was timid in making the double play. This did not go over well with new Twins manager Bill Rigney. It did not help matters when Rigney questioned Carew's courage in public.

Carew's injury probably cost him another batting title. He was hitting .376 when he was injured. When he returned to the lineup in September, he slumped a bit and finished the season at .366. That would have been good enough to win the batting crown, but he did not have enough plate appearances to qualify.

The Twins won the AL East title again in 1970, but in a repeat performance of 1969, they lost to the Orioles in three straight games in the AL Championship Series.

Carew's personal life changed in 1970 when he married Marilynn Levy, whom Rod had met two years earlier. This marriage of a black Episcopalian from Panama and a white Jewish woman from North Minneapolis was accepted by both sets of parents without protest, but not entirely by the Minneapolis community.

"We got death threats," said Marilynn Carew, "threats from people who felt what we did was their business. My mother got calls from people saying, 'How could your daughter do this?' They were going to shoot Rod at second base. They must have thought we were trying to prove something. We weren't. We weren't crusaders. We were just two people who met in a bar and happened to fall in love."

Despite his early success, Carew was not initially popular with Minnesota fans. He was often criticized in the media for his temperamental outbursts, and the fans often got down on him for what they perceived to be a lack of hustle. However, Carew was often very hard on himself. One time, when he failed to run hard after a ball he thought was foul but suddenly was blown into fair territory by a gust of wind, he immediately fined himself.

As the batting titles began to grow, so did his popularity. He became a hero in Minnesota, although he never liked the ceremony that went with fame. An extremely sensitive and introverted person, Carew nevertheless was well liked by his teammates and was always willing to help young players.

Carew won four consecutive batting titles from 1972 to 1975, but before the 1975 season began, he encountered his first major disagreement over money with Twins owner Calvin Griffith. Carew asked for a raise to $140,000 following a 1974 season in which he led the AL in batting with a .364 mark. Griffith refused, and Carew took the matter to salary arbitration. He lost. Griffith argued that Carew was merely a singles hitter and could not produce the long ball. He pointed out that Carew hit only three home runs during the 1974 season. The arbitrator agreed and awarded Carew $120,000, which made him vastly underpaid, considering his accomplishments.

Carew's pride was hurt by Griffith's accusations, and so the next year, just to prove to his boss that he could indeed hit home runs, he belted 14. He also won his fifth batting title in a row with a .359 average.

In 1976, Carew was moved from second base to first base, and the move was better for him and the Twins. It took some of the strain off Carew's weak knee, and it gave the Twins an opportunity to play someone at second who was better at turning the double play.

Rod "slumped" a bit to .331 in 1976 but drove in a career-high 90 runs and also had 200 hits for the third time in four seasons. During the season, he agreed to a three-year contract extension for $170,000 per season, even though many players not as good as he were making much more money by entering the free-agent market.

"I'm relaxed in Minnesota," he said. "I didn't want to risk not being relaxed somewhere else."

His feelings were soon to change, however. In 1977, Carew put together a season that he would never again duplicate. He made a major assault on the .400 mark, a feat that had not been achieved since Ted Williams hit .406 in 1941. Carew finished the season at .388. If he had gotten eight more hits, he would have made it to .400.

Carew finished the year with 239 hits, the most since Bill Terry had 254 in 1930, and he won the batting title by 50 points—the widest margin of victory in history. He also led the league in runs scored (128) and triples (16), equaled his career high in home runs, and knocked in 100 runs for the first and only time of his career. His outstanding season earned him the AL MVP award.

Now it was becoming increasingly clear that Griffith was not going to be able to keep Carew much longer. At the close of the 1977 season, two of Minnesota's key players, Lyman Bostock and Larry Hisle, became free agents and signed elsewhere. Bill Campbell, a quality relief pitcher, had done the same thing the year before.

Carew knew the Twins could no longer contend for a pennant, and he longed to play for a contender plus get some long-term financial security for his family. He asked Griffith for a five-year contract, but the Twins' owner refused. The two were at an impasse, and Carew knew he would have to be traded if he were to achieve his goals.

Then, on September 28, 1978, Griffith sealed Carew's fate. Speaking at a Lions Club dinner in Waseca, Minnesota, Griffith said Carew was a "damn fool" for signing a Twins contract when he could make so much more elsewhere. Then, later in his speech, the Twins' owner said he had moved the franchise from Washington, D.C., to Minneapolis because "I found out you only had 15,000 blacks here . . . We came here because you've got good, hardworking white people here."

Carew, who had always been on friendly terms with Griffith, was very upset by the remarks. "I'm not going to be another nigger on his plantation," Carew said.

The two men patched up their differences soon afterwards.

"We talked about it," said Carew. "It was just an unfortunate thing. He meant it one way and it came out the other. He'd always signed black players, and he'd always treated us well. I told him that as far as I was concerned, it was all forgotten. I kind of regretted making any comment at all about what he said."

Money, however, was still an issue. "He couldn't pay me, and I knew he couldn't," said Carew.

Griffith knew he would have to trade Carew or risk losing him to free agency and getting nothing in return. Since Rod had veto power over any trade, he could practically dictate anywhere he wanted to go. The Giants were interested, but Rod said no. The Angels wanted him and Carew was agreeable, but Griffith did not like the players California was offering. The Yankees came calling, and Griffith liked the players they were offering, but Carew did not want to play for Yankee owner George Steinbrenner.

Finally, the Angels came up with a package that was acceptable. On February 3, 1979, Carew was traded to the Angels for pitchers Paul Hartzell and Brad Havens, outfielder Ken Landreaux, and infielder Dave Engle. Carew signed a five-year contract for more than $4 million. He finally had his security.

Unlike the Twins, the Angels were loaded with stars. Owner Gene Autry so wanted to have a world-championship team that he was willing to spend lavishly to get one. But, while the Angels won the AL West twice during Rod's seven years with the team, they never made it to the World Series. Baltimore eliminated them in 1979, and Milwaukee in 1982.

At first, Rod took a lot of heat from the fans for his failure to drive in runs, but he consistently batted over .300 and eventually became a fan favorite. The highlight of his years in California came on August 3, 1985, in his final big-league season, when he collected his 3,000th hit. Fittingly, it was a slicing single to the opposite field off Carew's old team, the Twins, and it came against one of the game's best left-handers, Frank Viola.

Teammate Gary Pettis then paid Carew the ultimate compliment: "Most guys hit when they can—he hits when he wants to."

Five years after his retirement, Carew was paid the ultimate honor. He was elected to the Hall of Fame in his first year of eligibility.

Lou Brock

Ranking: 24th
Hit Total: 3,023

AP/Wide World Photos

L ou Brock took a short lead off first base and the crowd began to chant his name.

"Lou, Lou, Lou!" they shouted in unison. "Go, go, go!" the crowd implored.

Dave Freisleben, the pitcher for the San Diego Padres, threw to first, but Brock was back easily.

Freisleben again nervously eyed the runner. This time he delivered a pitch to the plate, but it did not count. Brock had called time. He had heard a voice.

"What?" he asked first-base umpire Billy Williams. Williams hadn't said a word.

Brock checked with Padres first baseman Gene Richards. He hadn't said anything, either. Brock asked first-base coach Sonny Ruberto. He had not uttered a word.

"I know I heard something," Brock said.

The game resumed and Freisleben again eyed the runner. Then, as his eyes shifted toward home plate and he began his delivery, Brock took off for second. The year was 1977. He was 38 years old now and not as speedy as he once was. But this was a man who had made base stealing a science, and he knew the odds were with him as he began his race to beat the ball thrown by catcher Dave Roberts.

Earlier in the game, Roberts had tried to nail Brock on a steal attempt and had failed miserably, his throw sailing into center field and allowing the St. Louis Cardinals' outfielder to advance to third. As had happened so often, Brock's steal had triggered a three-run inning.

This time Roberts's throw was better, but still much too far to the right of second. As Brock began his slide, Padres shortstop Bill Almon reached for the *ball and tried a sweep tag. The two players bumped, and Almon was sent sprawling. Brock was called safe and had stolen his 893rd career base, breaking a 44-year-old record that had been set by the legendary Ty Cobb.*

As the crowd roared its delight, Brock leaned over to Almon to ask him if he was all right.

"He took me out like on a double play—he hit me pretty hard," said Almon. "He was afraid he'd spiked me. He asked me if I was okay. Here he is, he's just set the record and he's turning around and showing concern. That's just the type of person he is."

When Brock retold the story after the game about the voice that no one but he had heard, Cardinals publicist Marty Hendin had a thought.

"Maybe it was the ghost of Ty Cobb," Hendin said.

It couldn't have been. Cobb wouldn't have cared about Almon.

Louis Clark Brock was the antithesis of the man whose stolen-base records he broke during a 19-year career (1961-79). While Cobb was racist, truculent, profane, suspicious, and humorless, Brock was amiable, caring, thoughtful, polite, and tolerant. He also gave much of his free time to helping others, especially youth.

Although his own stolen-base records were eventually erased by Rickey Henderson, Brock took the stolen base to a new level, following in the footsteps forged by Maury Wills of the Los Angeles Dodgers in the early 1960s.

As the leadoff batter for the Cardinals from 1964 to 1979, the left-handed-hitting Brock was the spirit of St. Louis. He collected 3,023 hits, led the league in stolen bases eight times, batted .300 or better eight times, and scored 100 or more runs in six seasons.

He was even more devastating to opponents in World Series competition. He stole seven bases in each of the 1967 and 1968 World Series, and his total of 14 ties Eddie Collins for the most in World Series competition. Brock holds the highest batting average (.391) among players with at least 20 World Series games. Even more remarkable is the fact that of the 23 hits he collected in World Series play, 13 of them were for extra bases.

Although slightly built at 5-11, 172 pounds, Brock had extraordinary power. He posted double figures in home runs in six seasons, and during his rookie year of 1962 with the Chicago Cubs, he became the only left-handed batter ever to hit a ball into the right-center-field bleachers of New York's Polo Grounds, a distance estimated at 488 feet.

Yet, despite his many contributions, he was in many ways not a quintessential leadoff batter. He struck out more than 100 times in nine seasons, and his on-base percentage was a rather ordinary .344. He finished with a lifetime batting average of .293 but is one of only five members of the 3,000 hit club not to have a lifetime batting average of .300 or better.

It was what Brock did when he was on base that made him such a dynamic presence. He stole 938 bases, and in the 1974 season swiped 118, which, at the time, was the most ever recorded in a single campaign. Henderson has since eclipsed both of those marks.

Brock had the ability to disrupt the concentration of opponents and demoralize a pitcher and a catcher so that they were no longer in sync. Although he never won a Most Valuable Player award during his big-league career, there were many on the Cardinals who believed Brock was the catalyst of the club.

Hall of Famer Willie Stargell, a slugging star for the Pittsburgh Pirates, remembered a game when pitcher Luke Walker was trying to keep Brock close to first.

"There were two things about Luke," said Stargell. "He had a terrible move to first, and you never were sure where the ball would go when he threw it.

"Lou, of course, knew that. So he takes one of the biggest leads off first I've ever seen, and I say, 'Lou, please come back here. Luke's gonna look over and he's gonna throw it right over my head.'

"Lou just smiled, and here comes Luke's throw—down into the bullpen and Lou's on third base. A couple of innings later and the same thing. I say, 'Lou, PLEASE come back.' Down into the bullpen again. Over to third again."

Brock on base was a pitcher's nightmare, yet the fleet outfielder took a different approach to stealing than many of his predecessors. He would take movies of opposing pitchers' deliveries and study them for hours, trying to detect one little flaw that might help him get a better jump. He also would take a stopwatch to catchers' throws, trying to decipher how much time elapsed from the moment the ball left the pitcher's hand until the throw got to second base.

Brock was unique among base stealers in that he did not take a big lead and favored a straight-in slide as opposed to a hook slide, preferred by Wills, or a headfirst slide, favored by Henderson.

"By taking a shorter lead and looking relaxed, my body is telling the pitcher I'm not going to run," said Brock. "Standing there, relaxed, upright, I'm causing doubts. All people who sprint start from a low position. The pitcher associates a low stance with running. He's conditioned to believe it's impossible to run from a straight-up position. I do."

His use of the straight-in, or pop-up, slide minimized contact with the ground, thereby lessening the wear and tear on his body, and it permitted him to advance quickly to third base on an overthrow.

While stealing bases became his trademark, he never chose that path. Instead it was chosen for him when he went to St. Louis from the Chicago Cubs in 1964.

"It was the club's philosophy that we were going to be a scratching, scrambling, gutty type of team," Brock said. "The question then became, 'Who's going to carry this out?' I was chosen.

"Stealing bases was put to me almost as a prerequisite for staying in the game. They didn't give me a handbook on how to do it; they said do it. Under those conditions, you go out and develop your own handbook."

Using his brain always came naturally to Brock. Born in El Dorado, Arkansas, on June 18, 1939, Brock grew up in Collinswood, Louisiana, and found out early that he excelled in the classroom.

"I was always academically oriented," he said. "It was a matter of pride and self-esteem. You don't want to be the dumbest kid in the school. Not the smartest necessarily, but not the dumbest. It was a competitive thing. I wanted to be able to hold my own in a crowd. At my high school, Union High in Mer Rouge, Louisiana, I'd represent the school in math and science competition as well as in baseball."

Raised by his mother, who gave birth to nine children by three husbands, Brock earned a partial scholarship to Southern University in Baton Rouge. He majored in math and sought to study architectural engineering, but he lost his scholarship after the first semester, and with that, went some jobs he had on campus.

He decided to try out for the baseball team in his second semester, but the coach ignored him and would not give him a chance to bat. All he would let Brock do was chase fly balls. Finally, after running around all day in the hot sun, Brock collapsed from exhaustion. The trainer revived him with smelling salts, and as a goodwill gesture, the coach let him hit.

"I took five swings and hit four out of the park," Brock recalled. "I made the starting lineup as a freshman and got an athletic scholarship my second year. All I really wanted to do was stay in school."

Brock, however, was soon discovered by the baseball scouts. Several scouts had come to Baton Rouge to look at a pitcher named Johnny Berry from Wiley College. He was pitching against Southern and took a no-hitter into the ninth inning. But Brock homered in the ninth to tie the score, 1-1, and two innings later, he homered again to give Southern a 2-1 victory.

"I was sporting a .500 average at the time, and the scouts started to ask who this kid was," said Brock.

In 1959, he got his first taste of big-time athletics by playing for the U.S. team in the Pan American Games. It was there he met Charles "Deacon" Jones, a track star. Jones was impressed with Brock's raw speed and suggested he might improve it with some technique. Later, when Brock was a rookie with the Cubs and Jones was employed as a salesman for the Humble Oil Co. in Chicago, the two worked out regularly together. Occasionally, they were joined by the great Olympic star Jesse Owens, and it was through the coaching of Jones and Owens that Brock learned economy of motion.

Brock dropped out of college after his junior year to sign a contract with the Cubs. He received $30,000 to be spread over several years. Although he wanted an education, he couldn't pass up the opportunity to give professional sports a try.

"Sports, I decided, was a young-man's game, so I took the chance," said Brock. "I knew I had something to fall back on. I had only one year to go in school, so if I fell flat on my face in baseball, the other was still attainable."

Brock spent only one year in the minor leagues, hitting .361 and stealing 38 bases for the Cubs' farm team in St. Cloud, Minnesota. In 1962, he was starting in left field for the Cubs. However, he was not happy. He considered himself a power hitter, an opinion given some support by that tremendous home run he hit at the Polo Grounds. But the Cubs envisioned him as a leadoff hitter, one who could use his speed to set the table for sluggers like Ernie Banks, Billy Williams, and Ron Santo.

The problem was Brock struck out too much. He fanned 96 times in 434 at-bats in 1962 and whiffed 122 times in 547 appearances the following year. He also was not an accomplished outfielder, nor had he begun to show his prowess as a base stealer. In two full seasons with the Cubs, he stole only 40 bases.

The Cubs and Brock were at a crossroads midway through the 1964 season when the Cardinals, who were searching for a leadoff hitter, inquired about obtaining the young speedster. They were willing to part with Ernie Broglio, a right-handed pitcher who won 21 games in 1960 and 18 in 1963. St. Louis also was willing to throw in 39-year-old left-hander Bobby Shantz and outfielder Doug Clemens.

Chicago jumped at the offer and agreed to give the Cardinals pitchers Paul Toth and Jack Spring along with Brock. It turned out to be one of the worst trades in the history of the game for Chicago. Broglio came down with a sore arm shortly after the trade and was out of baseball two years later. Yet, at the time, it appeared the Cubs had gotten the better of the deal.

"The Cubs got a 20-game winner for a guy with a tag reading 'maybe,'" said Brock. "And Clemens was my age and hitting just as well. There was no proof that either Clemens or I would come around, so anytime you can get a bona fide winning pitcher for a guy who hasn't done much, it looks like a good deal."

Johnny Keane, the manager of the Cardinals at the time, was the key man in engineering the trade. Even though Brock had hit only .263 and .258 in his two seasons with the Cubs, Keane liked his combination of speed and power and urged general manager Bing Devine to make the deal.

"We both liked Brock's speed and, I might add, his power. After all, he'd hit that home run at the Polo Grounds. But we had no way of knowing then that he'd become one of the all-time record breakers, a Cardinal in the class of Bob Gibson and Stan Musial," said Devine.

The Cardinals felt Brock could do for them what Wills had done for the Dodgers. Wills had broken Cobb's single-season record of 96 stolen bases by stealing 104 during the 1962 season. That year he also scored 130 runs and won the league's Most Valuable Player award, even though the Dodgers were beaten out for the pennant by the Giants in a playoff.

Initially, Brock thought asking him to steal was a put-down.

"The ultimate insult to me was saying I had to steal bases," said Brock. "It was put to me as an ultimatum that if I wanted to play regularly, I had to steal bases."

And did he ever. From 1965 through 1976, he stole 50 or more bases in each season, a major league record.

Brock's impact on the Cardinals was dramatic. He hit .346 and stole 33 bases over the final three months of the 1964 season and helped St. Louis eke out the pennant in an exciting stretch run. He hit .300 and knocked in five runs in the World Series as the Cardinals edged the New York Yankees, four games to three.

Brock helped St. Louis to another world championship in 1967. He hit .414 and stole seven bases as the Cardinals beat the Boston Red Sox in seven games. In 1968, Brock led the NL in doubles, triples, and stolen bases, a feat not accomplished since the great Honus Wagner did it in 1908.

The Cardinals won the pennant again in '68, and Lou had another spectacular World Series, collecting a record-tying 13 hits, including six for extra bases, and stealing another seven bases. But the Cardinals blew a three-games-to-one lead to Detroit and lost in seven games.

The 1968 season marked the Cardinals' last trip to the World Series during Brock's career. Yet, he brought an electricity to the game for another decade.

Even in his final season of 1979, at the age of 40 and with his speed just about gone, Brock went out in style. After struggling through his worst season (.221) in 1978, he rebounded to hit .304 in 120 games. Moreover, he had 123 hits, which enabled him to join the 3,000 hit club. Fittingly, perhaps, the historic 3,000th hit came against the Cubs.

"It (3,000 hits) symbolizes a lot of things," Brock said on the night he joined the 3,000 hit club. "It symbolizes longevity and success. As a lead-off man, which I have been, your ability to go from one base to another forces the pitchers to pitch tougher to you."

What Brock was saying was that pitchers often bore down harder against him, because if he got on base, it meant almost a certain double. As a result, a goodly number of his 3,000 hits were hard earned.

Retirement came easily to Brock. He kept busy in business with a company he had started early in his career. The company manufactured and marketed hat-like umbrellas, called Broccabrellas, which Lou redesigned from an early invention. He also did some baseball broadcasting.

In 1985, he reached the pinnacle of his baseball achievements by being elected to the Hall of Fame in his first year of eligibility.

Rafael Palmeiro

Ranking: 25th
Hit Total: 3,020

A ccording to legend, when the "Black Sox" scandal broke in 1920, Chicago's star outfielder "Shoeless" Joe Jackson was leaving the courtroom after it became known that he and seven of his teammates conspired to throw the 1919 World Series.

A youngster came up to Jackson, shocked and saddened, and begged of his hero, "Say it ain't so, Joe. Say it ain't so!"

Jackson simply looked down at the young man and said, sadly, "It's so, son. It's so."

Sometimes a good player gets stuck in a bad organization. Such was the case of Palmeiro. The Chicago Cubs, who made Palmeiro their number one draft pick in 1985, often seemed to focus more on what a player couldn't do than on what he could, and Chicago believed that Palmeiro first, wasn't fast enough for left field and second, didn't hit for enough power to play first base.

It made little sense at the time; as a twenty-three-year-old playing his first regular season, Palmeiro hit .307 with 41 doubles and made the NL All-Star team.

But then the Cubs weren't making good decision at that time. So, with young Mark Grace in their pipeline, Chicago traded Palmeiro to Texas in December 1987. While Grace was a fine player for Chicago, he didn't hit for power either, while Palmeiro developed into a steady and powerful presence in the American League.

Palmeiro, born in September 1964 in Cuba, immigrated to the United States as a child and became a star at Mississippi State University. Drafted out of college, he was starting in the majors by mid-1986. He was originally a contact hitter with doubles power but as he matured he added more home run sock.

In fact, a lot more home run sock. In 1991, Palmeiro hit 26 homers. In 1993, he leapt to 37. After signing as a free agent with the Orioles that December, he went on to club 182 long balls in five years for the Birds.

It is believed that sometime in that span, he began using steroids, which most analysts believed increased his power and staved off some of the natural decline a player experiences in his mid-to-late thirties. In the homer-happy game of the late 1990s and early 2000s, few people seemed to think it strange that Palmeiro could hit 47 homers at age thirty-six (after returning to Texas) and 43 more the following year.

Then again, it was a weird time. For all of Palmeiro's home-run artistry—he hit his 500th in 2003—he never led the league. In fact, Palmeiro never won a batting title and only once led the league in runs and hits. He was, all in all, a fine hitter in a time of elevated offense, but never one of the game's biggest stars. He never finished higher than fifth in any MVP voting, and only made four All-Star teams. He never played in a World Series. Rafael Palmeiro's twenty-year career was a testament to staying healthy and in the lineup, performing consistently, and being in good hitting environments.

Unfortunately, as Palmeiro's career wound down, what should have been his greatest time—the twilight of a star—instead became a bumpy road of lies, innuendo, and scandal.

In early 2005, Jose Canseco, in his book Juiced, "outed" Palmeiro as a steroid user and even claimed to have injected him personally. Called before a Congressional panel that March, Palmeiro stated, "Let me start by telling you this: I have never used steroids, period. I don't know how to say it any more clearly than that. Never."

On July 15, Palmeiro collected hit number 3,000 in Seattle, seemingly punching his ticket for the Hall of Fame with a double against Joel Piniero. That he tested positive for the steroid stanolozol just one month later was a sad and silly irony. During the remainder of the 2005 season—his last—Palmeiro endured heckling and boos wherever he went, bringing to an end a career that just months before been considered a shoo-in for Cooperstown.

It wasn't necessarily the use of steroids that bothered some fans as much as Palmeiro's condescending denials of such before a panel of the

United States Congress. Obviously there was little alternative for him.

Perhaps the saddest thing about it all is that Palmeiro may become only the second player to collect 3,000 hits not to be elected into the Hall of Fame.

Wade Boggs

Ranking: 26th
Hit Total: 3,010

AP/Wide World Photos

It was his first date with the woman who would one day become his wife, and Wade Boggs was in a predicament. Her car was not functioning well, and as she got within half a mile of Boggs's house, it broke down completely.

Now Boggs was in a near panic. It would be a while before any help would arrive to fix or tow the car, so he did what he felt he had to do. He got out of the car, said good night to his date, then sprinted for home, leaving his girlfriend stranded.

It was 15 minutes past his appointed bedtime and, as the future Mrs. Debbie Boggs would find out, strict routine and discipline were integral parts of this man's makeup.

So, too, were superstitions and idiosyncracies. Like eating chicken before every meal, or running wind sprints precisely at 7:17 p.m. before each night game, or drawing the Hebrew letter "chai," a symbol for good luck, in the batter's box before stepping up to the plate.

But habit and ritual are all part of growing up as the son of a Marine.

"Dinner was always at 5:30, and if you weren't home at 5:30, you didn't eat," Boggs recalled. "So you learned to always know where the clocks were in your friends' houses, and to this day I always notice clocks. I woke up at precisely the same time every day for 18 years. If I woke up, say, 30 minutes late, I was out of sync all day.

"From the time I was small, my pet peeve was being rushed, so I left for school at exactly the same time every day."

And, as Debbie Boggs knows full well, he went to bed at the same time every night.

All this attention to detail and routine might be construed by many as eccentric behavior, but then, Wade Anthony Boggs never really cared what people thought about him. He got his greatest pleasure from hitting a baseball, and few players in this last half century could hit as well as Boggs.

A left-handed batter who hit the ball to all fields with equal ability, Boggs is the only player in major league history to collect 200 or more hits in seven consecutive seasons (1983-89). He won five American League batting titles, scored 100 or more runs in a season seven straight years (1983-89), and batted .300 or better 15 times.

Not bad for a guy the scouts said would not make it to the big leagues because he was too slow, below average defensively, and couldn't hit for power.

Boggs spent the first 11 years of his big-league career with the Boston Red Sox, then spent five seasons with the New York Yankees before returning to his hometown of Tampa, Florida, to finish his career with the expansion Devil Rays.

Born on June 15, 1958, in Omaha, Nebraska, Boggs learned very early in life about the discipline of military life. His father, Win, was in the Marines in World War II. After leaving the corps in 1946, he worked at a variety of jobs until joining the Air Force at the outset of the Korean War. He served until 1967.

The family moved to Florida when Wade was very young, and he grew up in a hotbed of baseball, an area that produced major leaguers Fred McGriff, Steve Garvey, Lou Piniella, Dwight Gooden, and Gary Sheffield, among others.

Boggs was only 18 months old when his father took him out to the backyard and began pitching to him. He hit Wiffle balls, tennis balls, balls made of wine corks with tape wrapped around them, or practically anything that could be thrown.

Boggs was very particular about his approach to hitting right from the start. His father remembers taking him to a sporting goods store to find the right bat. Wade didn't find anything on the rack to his liking, so he rummaged through the stock rooms until he found bats with the right feel.

Later, when all of his teammates switched to aluminum bats, Wade stayed with the wooden ones. "I'd hit with wood since I was four years old, and they don't use aluminum in the big leagues," he said.

As a junior at H.R. Plant High School in Tampa, Boggs was the best hitter in Florida, batting .522 with eight homers and 41 RBI in 20 games. "For the first time in Wade's life, he took something for granted," said Win. "He thought it would be the same the next year, but I told him they'd pitch around him."

Win was right. After 10 games of his senior year, Wade was in the first slump of his life, with only four hits in 36 at-bats. It was after the 10th game that Win went to the Tampa Public Library and checked out Ted Williams's book, *The Science of Hitting*. Win told Wade he had four days to read the book and learn it. Wade did just that. He canceled a Saturday-night date with Debbie and studied the book all weekend.

"I realized I'd forgotten patience at the plate," Wade recalled. He learned his lessons well. In his last 11 games, he went 26-for-33 and finished at .485. He fully expected he would be taken in the June draft, and he hoped he would be selected in the first round.

He was wrong. He didn't go until the seventh round, when the Red Sox claimed him.

"There were a lot of people who liked him because he was a great hitter," said George Digby, a scout for the Red Sox, "but the Scouting Bureau representative came down, watched him for one game, and graded him a 25, which on their scale of 20 to 80 is about 13 points below the minimal level for a player to be drafted. The Dodgers and Reds liked him, but they backed off because they said he couldn't run. I just kept telling [Boston scouting director] Haywood Sullivan, 'Draft Boggs somewhere. Hitters like him don't come along often.'"

Boggs was devastated by his low selection. An all-state punter in football and an honor student, he had been offered a scholarship to the University of South Carolina, and he considered it. But when Digby showed up at his house the next morning and offered him $7,500 to sign with the Red Sox, Boggs jumped at the opportunity.

"I knew what I wanted," he said. "I knew the other scouts were wrong."

The Red Sox sent him to Elmira, New York, of the New York-Penn League, but he had trouble adjusting to professional pitching. Playing in 57 games, he hit only .263 with six extra-base hits. He also made 16 errors at third base.

That winter he married Debbie, and he began concentrating more on his hitting. He hit .332, .311, .325, and .306 over the next four years in stops at A, AA, and AAA. He also began to develop a reputation as somewhat of a flake because of his superstitions.

First, there was the protection that he gave his bats. He would carry them in a long, red bag and not let anyone near them. After the game, he would put them under lock and key. There was also the habit he had of using the bat to draw the Hebrew letter "chai" in the batter's box before stepping in to hit.

"I started that in high school," said Boggs. "I saw in a magazine that it was the Chinese sign for good luck. Turns out it's also the Hebrew sign for life."

His most publicized superstition was his penchant for eating chicken before every game. The habit was born in 1977, partly out of economy and partly out of personal preference, when Boggs was playing in Winston-Salem.

"You can't eat filet mignon on a minor league salary," said Boggs. When he began to hit well after feasting on chicken, it became a superstition.

"I noticed that I always seemed to hit best after chicken. So I started having Debbie fix it every day," he said. During his rookie season of 1982, he tried some of his mother's lemon chicken for the first time and went 7-for-9. Sure enough, it was added to his weekly regimen. In 1984, he and Debbie wrote a cookbook of chicken recipes with the clever title *Fowl Tips*.

After four successive seasons of hitting over .300 in the minor leagues, Boggs felt sure he would be called up to the big leagues for the 1981 season. But instead of adding him to the 40-man spring roster, the Red Sox made a trade with California for third baseman Carney Lansford. Boggs was eligible to be claimed by any team for $25,000, but there were no takers.

Boggs was placed on the roster of Boston's Triple A affiliate in Pawtucket, Rhode Island, for the 1981 season, and he went up to the manager, Joe Morgan, and asked him what he had to do to make the big leagues.

"Not many clubs are looking for a third baseman who is below average defensively, can't run, and doesn't hit for power," said Morgan. "You'll have to show more power."

Boggs thanked Morgan for his honesty and resolved to work 20 minutes a day in the field and half an hour driving the ball for power. The hard work paid off. He hit over .300 again for Pawtucket in 1981, and the following year he was in the major leagues.

Boggs opened the 1982 season on the Red Sox bench, but he took over at third base early in the season when Lansford suffered a sprained ankle. He made sure he was in the lineup to stay by hitting at a .390 clip over 25 games. When Lansford returned, Boston manager Ralph Houk shifted Boggs to first base and benched Dave Stapleton.

The switch to first was not completely foreign to Boggs. He had played the position and won MVP honors in Puerto Rico over the winter, and he handled it well. He finished the season as Boston's regular first baseman and hit .349 in 104 games.

Boggs did not demonstrate the power he had hoped for, as he hit only five home runs. But he did get rid of the tag that he was a poor fielder by performing well at both infield positions.

"I think I finally got the rap of 'all-hit, no-glove' off my back," said Boggs. "My next goal is to win a Gold Glove." He would eventually, but not for more than a decade later.

Boggs was not totally satisfied with his first season. He wanted to get stronger, so he began an off-season conditioning program to add muscle. It was during his training that he also found a way to improve his running speed.

"I always accepted that you can either run or you can't," said Boggs. "But one day during the winter after the '82 season, a couple of local track coaches watched me running, and one of them said, "Hey, you run all wrong. You run heel-toe. Run on the balls of your feet.' They showed me a program."

They told Boggs to get an inner tube, attach it to a wall in his basement, then, with the inner tube around his midriff, practice running against the tension of the strap every day. Boggs followed their advice and watched his running speed increase dramatically.

Lansford was gone after the 1983 season, and Boggs, stronger and faster than he had been the previous season, claimed the third-base job outright. He hit .361 to win his first batting title and also scored 100 runs for the first time. The Red Sox had themselves a bona fide star.

During 11 seasons with the Red Sox, Boggs proved to be one of the league's most durable players, as well as its premier hitter. From 1983 through 1992, Boggs never played fewer than 143 games in a season. He won four straight batting titles from 1985 to 1988, with his average never faltering below .357. In 1985, he collected 240 hits and reached base 340 times.

Despite his outstanding season in 1985, the Red Sox were only 82-82. That winter, Boggs became eligible for salary arbitration and submitted a figure of $1.8 million. The club countered with an offer of $1.35 million. Boggs, despite having won the batting title and scoring 107 runs, lost, as the arbitrator ruled in favor of the Red Sox. Boggs was bitter when he reported to spring training in 1986.

"It got a little better once I tried to forget about it and go about my business," he said. "But when you get 240 hits and hit .368 and people say you don't contribute, you got to have some doubts about whatever you do."

The 1986 season turned out to be one of great pain for Boggs in more ways than one. It started with great physical pain when he cracked a rib while taking off his cowboy boots in a Toronto hotel room on June 9. He was still suffering from the rib injury when he received news on June 16 that his mother, Sue Nell Boggs, had been killed in a traffic accident in Tampa.

Boggs left for a week, and when he returned, he found he could not concentrate.

"Baseball became secondary. I really didn't want to be out there," Boggs recalled. "I didn't care, and that's not me—me, the perfectionist. Even when I made outs, I didn't care. It was a total month of disbelief and wondering where I am.

"I finally turned it around. I talked with a lot of people, and that helped because I had gone out of the cocoon and didn't know where I was. I had no concentration, no inner feeling. I had to get back into the cocoon."

In August, manager John McNamara moved him into the leadoff position, and Boggs was not pleased. He had lost his arbitration hearing because the team said he did not drive in runs. How was he going to drive in runs from the leadoff spot?

But Boggs bit his lip and played, and the team prospered from the switch. With Boggs hitting .357 and driving in 71 runs, the Red Sox won the American League East title. They defeated the California Angels in a heart-stopping AL Championship Series for the right to meet the New York Mets in the World Series.

The Red Sox had not won a World Series since 1918, but they entered Game 6 needing only one more victory to secure the championship. The two teams battled to a 3-3 tie through nine innings, then the Red Sox scored twice in the 10th to take a 5-3 lead. They got the first two outs in the last of the 10th and were only a strike away from victory when one of the most colossal collapses in baseball history occurred. Three straight singles, a wild pitch, and an error gave the Mets an improbable victory to even the Series. The Mets won the next day, too, after coming back from a 3-0 deficit.

It was as close to a world championship as Boggs would get with the Red Sox. The team won AL East titles in 1988 and 1990, but each time was swept in three games by the Oakland A's in the AL Championship Series.

In 1988, Boggs' reputation was sullied somewhat when he became embroiled in a suit with a California woman named Margo Adams, who sued him for palimony. The suit produced some awkward moments for Boggs and his family. It was soon forgotten by the public, after Boggs hit .366 to win his fifth batting title.

Boggs remained with the Red Sox through the 1992 season, then joined the Yankees as a free agent. He hit better than .300 for four straight seasons with the Yankees, won a Gold Glove in 1995, and earned his only World Series ring in 1996. A picture of Boggs riding on the back of a policeman's horse, holding his index finger up to the sky after the deciding game, is an indelible memory of that Series.

After the 1997 season, he signed with the expansion Tampa Bay Devil Rays as a free agent. He hit .280 in 123 games for Tampa Bay in 1998 and joined the 3,000 hit club with them on August 7, 1999, with a home run off Chris Haney of Cleveland. Boggs, who had three hits on that day to reach the milestone, is the only member of the 3,000 hit club to join the club with a home run.

The final chapter to Boggs's career will be written on the day he is elected to the Hall of Fame, which will come in his first year of eligibility.

Al Kaline

Ranking: 27th
Hit Total: 3,007

AP/Wide World Photos

Cleveland's Dale Mitchell hit a sinking line drive to right field that appeared to be a sure hit. Detroit's right fielder, Al Kaline, raced in to make a shoestring catch but couldn't quite make the play. The ball hit off Kaline's glove and rolled a few feet away as the Tigers' right fielder went sprawling on the grass. Mitchell spotted the ball on the ground and took off for second base. Kaline, realizing he had no time to get to his feet and throw, picked the ball up and threw a bullet to second base from a sitting position to nail Mitchell. Players from both benches shook their heads in amazement.

In another game, at Yankee Stadium, the Tigers were leading by one run, but the Yankees were threatening with two on and two out in the last of the ninth. Mickey Mantle, the Yankees' top slugger, then hit a ball so hard that Mel Allen's broadcasting assistant yelled into the microphone, "The Yankees win five to four."

In the Detroit clubhouse, the equipment manager angrily flipped off the radio and waited for the Tigers to trudge in with their heads down. Instead, they were laughing and shouting as they entered the clubhouse. Kaline had raced to the auxiliary scoreboard, supported himself with his bare right hand against the wall, leaped and twisted high in the air, and caught the ball back-handed to end the game.

When the game was on the line, Tigers' fans knew they could count on "The Line," a nickname Boston's colorful relief pitcher John Wyatt pinned on Kaline.

One of the best all-around players in baseball during the 1950s and 1960s, Al Kaline played 22 seasons in the major leagues, all of them with the Detroit Tigers, and collected 3,007 hits while batting .297. He is the youngest player ever to win a batting title, compiling a .340 average in 1955 at the age of 20. He also led the league in hits once, doubles once, and slugging percentage once.

Curiously, however, Kaline's career as an offensive player fell short of expectations. He won a batting title at the age of 20 but never won another. He never led the American League in either home runs or RBI, never hit 30 homers in a season, managed 200 hits only once, and never won a Most Valuable Player award.

Still, he was the Tigers' franchise player for two decades and was unsurpassed as a defensive player. He won 10 Gold Gloves and earned a reputation as one of the best clutch players in the game.

He also stood out among his peers in the All-Star Games. Kaline played in 16 of them and hit .324 with two home runs.

One wonders what he might have accomplished had his career been injury-free, like those of Willie Mays, Hank Aaron, and Stan Musial. But Kaline was often hurt and averaged fewer than 130 games a season for his career. Like Mickey Mantle, Kaline suffered from osteomyelitis, a bone disease. When he was eight years old, doctors took two inches of bone out of his left foot, leaving jagged scars and permanent deformity.

During his career, Kaline had an inordinate number of broken bones— a broken cheekbone in 1959, a broken collarbone in 1962, a broken finger in 1967, and a broken right arm in 1968. Then there was a rib injury in 1965 and a foot malformation resulting in an operation in 1965.

Each time, though, Kaline bounced back like an All-Star. Even in 1968, when the broken arm limited him to 102 games, Kaline came back to hit .379 and drive in eight runs in the Tigers' World Series victory over the St. Louis Cardinals.

Some say Albert William Kaline was born to play baseball. He certainly was guided into it. Born on December 19, 1934, in Baltimore, Maryland, Kaline grew up in a baseball family. His father, Nicholas; his uncles Bib and Fred; and his grandfather Philip had all been semipro catchers from the Eastern Shore of Maryland.

When he was six years old, he was so good that he was permitted to shag flies and warm up pitchers for the noon softball games that were played by the gas and electric company down the street from his house. At 11, he set an elementary school record by throwing a softball 173 feet, 6 inches. When the judges did not believe what they'd just witnessed, Kaline repeated the feat.

As a pitcher in a league for 10- to 12-year-olds, Kaline went 10-0. When he got to high school, the coach thought he was too small to be a pitcher, and so he cut him from the team. Kaline again tried to make it—

this time as a second baseman—but was cut once more. When one of the outfielders got hurt, Kaline finally got a chance to play, and he didn't disappoint. In four years as a regular in high school, he posted batting averages of .333, .418, .469, and .488 and made the All-Maryland team each year, a feat last accomplished by slugger Charlie Keller, who went on to fame with the New York Yankees.

The Kaline family was poor, but they sensed young Al had a chance to be a big-league ballplayer. So they entered him in every league imaginable. On Sundays he would play in two and sometimes three games, with his father and uncles shuttling him from game to game while he changed uniforms in the car. In one league, Al hit .609, and he eventually caught the eye of a Tigers scout.

By the time he signed with the Tigers at 18 for a $30,000 bonus, he had played in more games than many players five years older.

"I suffered a lot as a kid playing in all those games," Kaline recalled. "You know how Baltimore is real hot in the summer? When everybody was going on their vacations, going swimming with all the other kids, here I was Sundays playing doubleheaders and all because I knew I wanted to be a ballplayer and my dad always told me, 'You're gonna have to work hard, and you're gonna have to suffer if you're gonna be a ballplayer. You're gonna have to play and play all the time.'

"There was a couple of times when I told my dad I wasn't gonna play Sunday, I was gonna go down to the beach with my girl or with a bunch of the guys to go swimming. And he says, 'Now look, like I told you in the beginning when you agreed to play for these people, they're gonna be counting on you, so if you're not gonna play, tell 'em to tear your contract up.' So I would go play, but it was these things he did to me that showed me the right way and pushed me the right way."

All the hard work paid off when the Tigers signed him to a contract, and he immediately gave the first $15,000 to his father. It helped the Kaline family pay off the mortgage on their house and enabled Al's mother to get an operation that saved her eyesight.

Kaline was thrust right into the pressure cooker of the major leagues. He never played a game in the minors. His first big-league manager was Fred Hutchinson, and he made a strong impact on the young outfielder.

Shortly after arriving in Philadelphia for his first big-league game, Kaline was summoned to Hutchinson's room. He went there without unpacking his suitcase.

"You'll sit next to me on the bench, Al," Hutchinson said. "I'll keep telling you what you need to do to be a major leaguer."

The date was June 25, 1953, and Hutch let Kaline play the last two innings in center field as a replacement for Jim Delsing.

"I had my first time at bat in the game," recalled Kaline. "Harry Byrd was pitching and did he ever look big to me. I figured he was at least 6-4 and 230 pounds. They tell me he never got that big, but I don't know."

Kaline swung at Byrd's first pitch and flied out to center field. Before the end of the season, he managed seven hits, including the first of 399 career home runs, in 28 at-bats for a .250 average.

Kaline began the 1954 season on the bench, but starting right fielder Steve Souchock broke his arm early in the season, and Hutchinson put Kaline in right. In one of his early games, Kaline showed off his powerful arm by throwing out three Chicago base runners in successive innings. He cut down Fred Marsh trying to score from second on a single, threw out Minnie Minoso trying to stretch a single into a double, and nailed Chico Carrasquel attempting to go from first to third on a single.

While players from both teams marveled at his powerful arm, Kaline took it all in stride.

"I was there because I was a fielder," he said. "That's what kept me in the league. The question was: Did I have enough bat?"

Kaline answered that question in his second major league season. In 1955, at the age of 20, he hit .340 to become the youngest player ever to win a batting crown. In a game against Kansas City that year, he hit three home runs, including two in one inning. Some baseball people began comparing him to the legendary Tiger great Ty Cobb. *The Sporting News* named him the Player of the Year.

Yet, although he would post eight more .300-plus seasons, he never came close to winning another batting title, and this mistakenly caused many fans to look at his career as unfulfilled promise.

"The worst thing that ever happened to me in the big leagues was the start I had," said Kaline during a 1964 interview. "This put the pressure on me. Everybody said this guy's another Ty Cobb, another Joe DiMaggio. How much pressure can you take? What they didn't know is that I'm not that good a hitter. They kept saying I do everything with ease. But it isn't that way. I have to work as hard, if not harder, than anybody in the league.

"I'm in spring training a week early every year. I've worked with a heavy bat in the winter to strengthen my hands. I've lifted weights, done push-ups, but my hitting is all a matter of timing. I don't have the kind of strength that Mantle or Mays have, where they can be fooled on a pitch and still get a good piece of the ball. I've got to have my timing down perfect or I'm finished."

In the first few years after he won the batting championship, Kaline went into frequent depressions over his inability to give the fans what he new they expected from him. After each game, he would sit in front of his locker and not say a word. He would often appear sullen and moody to newspapermen.

"But I didn't really sulk, the way the newspapermen said I did," Kaline said. "I was just quiet, and when a newspaperman came up to me and said, 'Nice game,' or something like that, I'd just say, 'Thank you.' I would never prolong the conversation, and the guys who didn't know me would say, 'Look at this stuck-up kid.' But it was just my way. I don't talk much. I don't like to make people mad at me, and if you talk too much, you're gonna put your foot in your mouth sooner or later."

The Tigers' front office also put pressure on Kaline to be more colorful. But that was like asking a tiger to change its stripes.

"They told me to be more colorful, that I could bring more people into the ballpark if I was more colorful," said Kaline. "But how could I do that? I could jump up and down on the field and make an ass out of myself for arguing with umpires, but I'm not made that way. I could make easy catches look hard, but I'm not made that way, either."

Although he never won a batting title after 1955, Kaline certainly gave Detroit fans more to cheer about than most other players who made their way through the Tiger system. In fact, the year after winning the batting crown, he had perhaps an even better year, when he hit .314 with 27 homers and 128 RBI.

From 1954 through 1963, he hit over .300 seven times, hit 25 or more homers six times, and drove in 90 or more runs six times. He also led AL outfielders twice in assists during those years. In 1963, he again was named Player of the Year by *The Sporting News* after hitting .312 with 27 homers and 101 RBI.

"Al has all the qualities you look for in a player," Detroit manager Mayo Smith said of Kaline during the 1970 season. He can beat you with the long ball, with the stolen base, and with his glove and arm. What more do you need to say? He just keeps going on and on. His class never dims."

"When you talk about all-around ballplayers, I'd say Kaline was the best I ever played against," said Brooks Robinson of the Baltimore Orioles.

One thing that bothered Kaline the most during his career was the Tigers' failure to win more pennants. The Tigers appeared in the World Series only once (1968) in Kaline's 22 seasons. Detroit won the AL East title in 1972 but was beaten by the Oakland Athletics in the playoffs.

Kaline went through 14 managers during his career, and Smith was the only one to produce a pennant and subsequent World Series championship. Not surprisingly, Kaline was the batting star of that World Series.

He had suffered a broken arm when hit by A's pitcher Lew Krausse during the 1968 season and managed to get only 327 at-bats. But he returned as a first baseman down the stretch and helped the Tigers to 103 victories. He went back to the outfield in the World Series, and when the Tigers fell behind, three games to one, Kaline took charge.

He rallied the Tigers from behind in Game 5 by singling in the tying and go-ahead runs. In Game 6, he singled twice in a 10-run third inning as the Tigers romped, 13-1. The Tigers also won Game 7, 4-1, and Al finished with a .379 average. He had two homers and two doubles among his 11 hits and knocked in a Series-high eight runs.

In 1972, injuries limited Kaline to only 278 at-bats, but he came on strong at the end of the season and helped the Tigers nip the Boston Red Sox by one game for the AL East pennant. In the playoffs, the Tigers lost a tough five-game series to the Athletics, with Al delivering a home run in a Game 1 loss and a clutch single in Game 4, which the Tigers won to square the series.

Although one of the game's most gifted outfielders, Kaline might never have reached the 3,000 hit milestone if it weren't for the designated-hitter rule, which was instituted in the AL in 1973.

Kaline entered the 1974 season needing 139 hits to reach 3,000. A weak left knee made it impossible for him to play in the outfield or even at first base. His body was wearing down, and he had made up his mind that he would retire once he reached 3,000 hits. Yet, it seemed unlikely that he could do it in 1974, since he had barely managed 139 hits in 1972 and 1973 combined.

But the designated-hitter rule proved the perfect remedy for Al's physical problems. He played in 147 games as the DH and managed 146 hits to finish the season with 3,007. Ironically, the historic 3,000th hit came in his hometown of Baltimore, a slicing double to right off Orioles left-hander Dave McNally.

"This definitely ranks above the batting championship," said Kaline. "Anytime you win a batting championship, there's a lot of luck that goes with it.

"But when you get 3,000 hits, I don't think anybody can say you were lucky. You've had to withstand the pressure of all those seasons and all the injuries and everything. To me, that really means something."

Kaline retired after the 1974 season and later became a broadcaster with the Tigers. While no Tiger uniform had been retired in deference to Ty Cobb, who didn't wear numerals, Kaline's No. 6 was taken out of circulation in August 1980 after his first-ballot election to the Hall of Fame.

Roberto Clemente

Ranking: 28th
Hit Total: 3,000

Courtesy of Pittsburgh Pirates

I t was the day before the 1971 World Series, and Roberto Clemente, star right fielder for the Pittsburgh Pirates, was eager for the battle with the Baltimore Orioles.

For too long he had toiled in obscurity, a black superstar in a mostly white, blue-collar city that was far removed from the media frenzy of New York, Chicago, or Los Angeles.

His greatest seasons, in the 1960s, were witnessed by some of the smallest crowds in history. Since there was no ESPN or TBS in those days, some of Clemente's most dazzling plays went unrecognized or unnoticed.

But the World Series was different. Now, he could showcase his talents before millions on national television. Now, they would see the great Clemente rise to the occasion.

He had played in a World Series before, in 1960, and had hit .310 against the New York Yankees. But he was a kid then, and the star that year was Bill Mazeroski, whose dramatic home run in the ninth inning of the seventh game won the Series for the Pirates.

Over the past decade Clemente, now 37, had evolved into one of the game's greatest all-around players. He could not wait to show the nation.

"Now they will see how I play," he said to a reporter. "Nobody does anything better than me in baseball."

Never has anyone been as true to his word. The Pirates won the World Series in seven games, and Clemente played like a man on a mission. He batted .414 with 12 hits in 29 at-bats, including two home runs, two doubles, and a triple. He ran the bases aggressively, played flawlessly in right field, and displayed rifle-armed throws that prevented runners from advancing. He was unquestionably the MVP.

"That Series was his personal deal," recalled Pirates pitcher Steve Blass, who won two games in the Series, including a four-hit shutout in Game 7. "It was his showcase, a chance to see what we in Pittsburgh had seen for a lot of years."

On the plane back to Pittsburgh after Game 7, Clemente sought out Blass, and the two embraced. It was an emotional moment that Blass never forgot. Fourteen months later, Roberto Clemente was dead.

Roberto Walker Clemente was one of the greatest all-around players in the game's history. A native of Puerto Rico, he was the first Latin superstar. During an 18-year (1955-72) career, he compiled a .317 batting average, won four National League batting championships, and earned 12 Gold Gloves. He also was one of the few players to win Most Valuable Player awards for both the regular season (1966) and the World Series (1971).

Clemente spent his entire career with the Pittsburgh Pirates and was the heart and soul of the team. A fiercely proud man, Clemente was not only one of the greatest players of his era, but he was also a humanitarian, a person concerned with other, worldly, issues outside the lighthearted life of major league baseball.

"He gave the term 'complete' a new meaning," former baseball commissioner Bowie Kuhn said of Clemente. "He made the word 'superstar' seem inadequate. He had about him the touch of royalty."

It was his concern for others that cost Clemente his life at the age of 38. He was killed on December 31, 1972, in the crash of a small plane that was taking relief supplies to earthquake-torn Nicaragua. His death came only three months after he collected his 3,000th and final major league hit.

"I want to be remembered as a ballplayer who gave all he had to give," Clemente once said. That one sentence would serve as his epitaph.

He certainly gave his all as a ballplayer. "He was the best all-around ballplayer I ever saw . . . without qualification," said his longtime manager, Danny Murtaugh.

Yet, for much of his career, Clemente played under a cloud. Bothered by a bad back for much of his career, the result of an auto accident in 1954, he played in pain but was often labeled a complainer and a hypochondriac by the news media.

"When he was hurt, he had trouble explaining himself because of the language problem, and everyone thought he was jakin' [malingering]." said Mazeroski in 1971. "I don't think he's ever jaked."

Willie Stargell, a Hall of Famer and former teammate, thinks the perception of Clemente as a hypochondriac is way off base.

"How are you going to get 3,000 hits if you're a hypochondriac?" said Stargell. "We faced Koufax, Drysdale, Gibson, Marichal, Perry, a young Seaver, Ryan, Carlton, and Jenkins. That's the kind of baseball we had to play. To have the success he had against that kind of talent, it's overwhelming.

"We got a chance to see a very special individual. As a teammate, we had a chance to marvel at talents a lot of people didn't understand."

Clemente was born on August 18, 1934, in Carolina, Puerto Rico. His father was a foreman at a sugar cane plantation, and his mother operated a grocery store and meat market for the plantation workers. From the time he was a small boy, he was instilled with a strong moral code and a love for both his heritage and his birthplace.

He began his athletic career as a softball player, and it was not until he was 17 that he got to play his first game of baseball. It became apparent right away that Clemente was a special baseball talent, and a scout for the Santurce professional team, Pedro Zorilla, saw Clemente play a few games and signed him to a contract in 1952 that included a $5,000 bonus. In the winter of 1952-53, Clemente hit .356 and began attracting the attention of American baseball scouts.

One of those scouts was Al Campanis of the Brooklyn Dodgers. Campanis saw Clemente at a clinic in Puerto Rico and came away so impressed that he offered him a $10,000 bonus to sign with the Dodgers when he graduated from high school. This was more money than the Dodgers had ever paid for a Latin player.

The Dodgers weren't sure what to do with Clemente, because they already had a veteran outfield. But Campanis was a shrewd judge of talent, and he knew that other teams would soon be attracted to Clemente. One of those teams was the Giants, and they already had a talented youngster named Willie Mays. Campanis wanted to take no chances that the Giants might also end up with Clemente.

As it was, the Milwaukee Braves came in with the best offer, a $30,000 bonus, but Clemente had already agreed to go with the Dodgers, and he kept his word.

Clemente, 19, was assigned to the Dodgers' Triple A club in Montreal in 1954. Under the rules of the time, however, a player receiving more than $4,000 and not assigned directly to the major league team contracting him could be drafted by another team after one year. Since the Brooklyn club was already loaded with talent and there was no room for Clemente, the Dodgers decided to "hide" him from other teams in hopes that he wouldn't be drafted.

The Dodgers accomplished this by having him bat almost exclusively against right-handed pitchers and using him sparingly. He got to bat only 148 times in 1954 and hit .257 with two home runs and 12 RBI.

"We figured he'd hit .120 and nobody would be interested," said E.J. "Buzzie" Bavasi, then the Dodgers' general manager. "He hit anyway. You can't hide the great ones."

Naturally, Clemente was bewildered by the Dodgers' refusal to play him much. "If I struck out, I stay in the lineup," he said. "If I played well, I'm benched . . . I didn't know what was going on, and I was confused and almost mad enough to go home. That's what they wanted me to do. That way nobody could draft me."

In Pittsburgh, former Dodgers GM Branch Rickey was now running the Pirates, and he knew all about Clemente. Rickey had sent scout Clyde Sukeforth to Montreal to watch Joe Black pitch in a game. The Pirates were considering a trade for Black, a former NL Rookie of the Year with Brooklyn. Sukeforth, though, wasn't impressed with Black, but he was with Clemente, who showed off his arm during pregame drills.

Sukeforth told Rickey that he thought Clemente had the potential to be a fine major league player, and he recommended the Pirates take him in the November draft. Since they had finished last in the NL the previous season, the Pirates had the first choice in the round-robin draft of eligible players.

Bavasi knew Rickey was familiar with Clemente's talent, and so he went and asked his old boss for a favor.

"When Mr. Rickey left for Pittsburgh, he wanted me to go along," said Bavasi. "I told him I wanted to stay with the Dodgers, and he said if there was ever anything he could do for me to let him know.

"I went to see Mr. Rickey and told him he owed me a favor. I said I was going to leave a young pitcher, John Rutherford, available for the draft and would appreciate it if the Pirates would take him instead of Clemente. Mr. Rickey agreed."

But the day before the draft at the NL meetings in New York, Rickey and Dodgers general manager Walter O'Malley got into an argument over money. Rickey was so mad at the Dodgers that he called Bavasi and told him the deal was off. The next day, the Pirates claimed Clemente with the first pick.

Clemente joined the Pirates in 1955 as the team's regular right fielder. He did not particularly impress at the plate in his first year, batting .255 with five home runs and 47 RBI in 124 games. He hit .311 the next year, but slumped to .253 in 1957 before rebounding with seasons of .289 and .296.

While he was still learning the nuances of hitting, he already was being heralded as one of the best defensive right fielders in the game. Along with some eye-opening catches, he displayed a cannon-like arm that became the scourge of the league. During his career, Clemente amassed 266 assists, the 18th most in major league history. Eventually, runners stopped trying to advance a base when the ball was hit to Clemente.

"Clemente could field the ball in New York and throw out a guy in Pennsylvania," Dodgers broadcaster Vin Scully said.

The turning point in Clemente's career came in 1960, the Pirates' championship season. He hit .314 with 16 home runs and 94 RBI during the regular season and collected nine hits in 29 at-bats for a .310 average in the seven-game Pirates' victory over the Yankees. He finished eighth in the NL MVP voting but believed in his heart that he should have won it.

"I was bitter," he said six years later. "I still am."

It was about that time that Clemente became very guarded in his dealings with the media He was careful with his words, not wanting what he said to be misinterpreted, although it often was. He understood that Pittsburgh was a small market, yet he believed he was overlooked in the media excitement over stars such as Mays and Hank Aaron.

From 1961 through 1965, he posted batting averages of .351, .312, .339, and .329. He won NL batting titles in 1961, 1964, and 1965. Then, in 1966, he reached the pinnacle by winning the MVP award after a season in which he hit .317 with 29 homers and 119 RBI. He won his fourth batting title a year later with a .357 average.

After the 1967 season, a national sports magazine conducted a poll of the major league general managers, asking them who they thought was the best player in baseball. Eight out of 18 picked Clemente. Carl Yastrzemski finished second with six votes, and four other players received one vote each.

A year after being named the best player in baseball, Clemente's back problems returned, and he hit only .291. He seriously considered retirement but decided to return. Early in the 1969 season, he suffered a shoulder injury and was batting only .200 after the first 27 games. But he bounced back to finish at .345, second to Cincinnati's Pete Rose in the race for the batting title.

With Clemente hitting .352, the Pirates won the NL East title in 1970 but were defeated by the Reds in the NL Championship Series. Sparked by Clemente's heroics, the Pirates won it all in 1971, and the Pirates' star found himself only 118 hits shy of 3,000.

Getting to the coveted mark was a struggle, however. Bothered by nagging injuries for the entire season, Clemente was in and out of the lineup, and as the season was drawing to a close in late September, it was beginning to look as if he might not reach his goal.

On September 29 against the New York Mets, he thought he had No. 3000 when he hit a high bouncer toward second baseman Ken Boswell. Boswell, however, bobbled the ball, and official scorer Luke Quay, who considered himself Clemente's No. 1 booster among sportswriters, charged the Mets' second baseman with an error.

Clemente was livid. Later he charged that official scorers throughout his career had deprived him of two batting titles.

The following day, Clemente got his 3,000th hit. It came in the fourth inning when he laced a double to left-center off Mets left-hander Jon Matlack. The crowd of 13,119 stood and cheered, and second-base umpire Doug Harvey presented the ball to Clemente.

"I dedicated the hit to the Pittsburgh fans and to the people in Puerto Rico and to one man in particular," Clemente said. "The one man who carried me around for weeks looking for a scout to sign me."

The man was Roberto Marin, a Puerto Rican who urged the Brooklyn Dodgers to sign Clemente in 1954.

Clemente's 3,000th hit would be his last. He had expected to return for the 1973 season, but in December an earthquake struck Nicaragua, and Clemente, always eager to lend a helping hand to people in need, volunteered his services to help fly supplies to the grief-stricken country.

He made one trip with supplies and conducted a clinic there. But he became concerned about how the supplies were being distributed and decided to make another trip. The second trip was arranged for New Year's Eve.

The plane chosen for the trip was a prop-driven DC-9. It was an old plane with a history of problems, but the flight had already been delayed 16 hours, and there was no time to look for a replacement plane. So five men, including Clemente, loaded 16,000 pounds of relief supplies onto the plane and took off for Nicaragua.

Sometime before midnight, the plane crashed into the icy sea. No bodies of the passengers were ever found. The world was crushed by the news of Clemente's death. Manny Sanguillen, a Pirates catcher from Puerto Rico who idolized Clemente, donned a wet suit and dove several times into the area where the plane went down, hoping to find Clemente's body and bring some closure to the incident. He could not.

Clemente's death made him more popular and respected in Pittsburgh and Puerto Rico than ever before. Hospitals, playgrounds, schools, and apartment complexes were named after him. He became known not only as a great baseball player, but as a great humanitarian and an icon, too.

The Baseball Writers Association of America, which votes on the Hall of Fame, waived the customary five-year waiting period and installed Clemente in Cooperstown in 1973. But the loss to those who knew him was staggering.

"He was one of those special people," said Stargell. "He touched a lot of people's lives. He was given the opportunity to do something, and he did it as well as he could. This is his legacy."

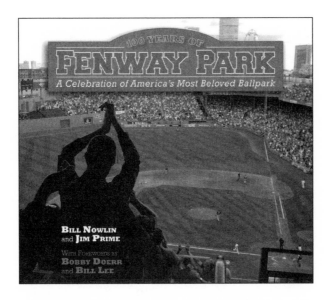

100 Years of Fenway Park

A Celebration of America's Most Beloved Ballpark

by Bill Nowlin and Jim Prime

Forewords by Bobby Doerr and Bill Lee

On April 20, 1912, The Boston Red Sox played their first official game at Fenway Park. Twenty-seven thousand fans were on hand to witness the Red Sox defeat the rival New York Highlanders, later known as the Yankees, 7–6 in 11 innings. It was an event that may have made front page news in Boston had it not been for the sinking of the *Titanic* five days earlier.

Since that day, the oddly-shaped stadium at 4 Yawkey Way has played host to nearly 8,000 Red Sox games, including fifty-five in the postseason, launching the legends of Tris Speaker, Jimmie Foxx, Ted Williams, Carl Yastrzemski, Jim Rice, Wade Boggs, and Pedro Martinez, and making the ballpark a worldwide destination for legions of baseball fans in the process.

From the Green Monster to Pesky's Pole, The Triangle to the lone red seat marking the longest home run ever hit in the stadium (a 502-foot blast off the bat of Ted Williams in 1946), Fenway Park's unique charms have captivated generations of sports fans. Through vivid full-color photographs and illuminating prose, *100 Years of Fenway Park* tells the story of the most cherished American stadium.

$29.95 Hardcover

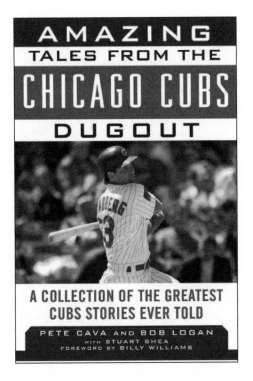

Amazing Tales from the Chicago Cubs Dugout
A Collection of the Greatest Cubs Stories Ever Told

by Pete Cava and Bob Logan

Foreword by Billy Williams

Amazing Tales from the Chicago Cubs Dugout is crammed with stories, quotes, and anecdotes about the greatest Cubs players of past and present. The story of the Cubs is part legend, part pathos; heroic and, on occasion, hilarious. Enjoy the heartbreak and joy of unforgettable afternoons at Wrigley Field. Without a doubt *Amazing Tales from the Chicago Cubs Dugout* is a must for any Chicago Cubs fan.

$24.95 Hardcover

ALSO AVAILABLE

The Baseball Maniac's Almanac

The Absolutely, Positively, and Without Question Greatest Book of Facts, Figures, and Astonishing Lists Ever Compiled

by Bert Randolph Sugar with Stuart Shea

An addictive read, sure to spark conversation wherever baseball is spoken, the third edition of *The Baseball Maniac's Almanac* is part reference, part trivia, part brain teaser, and absolutely the greatest, most unusual, and thorough compendium of baseball stats and facts ever compiled.

$14.95 Paperback

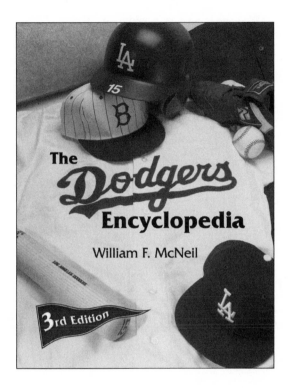

The Dodgers Encyclopedia

by William F. McNeil

The newly updated third edition of *The Dodgers Encyclopedia* is the definitive book on Brooklyn and Los Angeles Dodgers baseball. It traces the history of one of Major League Baseball's most successful organizations, from the fledgling beginnings of its predecessors in rural Brooklyn over 145 years ago, through their formative years in the major leagues. More than just a tome of facts, this book covers every important event with vivid detail—every no-hitter, every World Series, every tragedy and triumph of Dodgers baseball is captured in this fascinating reference. Within these pages, readers will also find biographies of over 100 of the best players to ever don the Dodgers uniform. Fans will find all their favorites, from the unbeatable James Creighton in 1860 to Sandy Koufax, Fernando Valenzuela, Mike Piazza, and more. Newly updated through the 2010–2011 season, *The Dodgers Encyclopedia* is a must-have for any Dodgers fan.

$24.95 Paperback

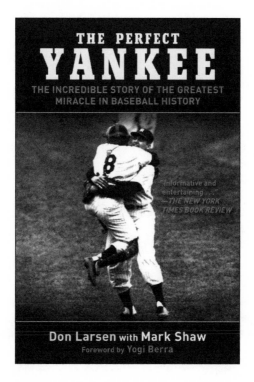

The Perfect Yankee

The Incredible Story of the Greatest Miracle in Baseball History

by Don Larsen and Mark Shaw

Foreword by Yogi Berra

It was one perfect moment, one singular feat unparalleled in the half a century of baseball that followed. It was Game 5 of the 1956 World Series. In an age when nobody spat in anyone's face, strikes were called only on the field, and New York was baseball's battlefield, Don Larsen pitched the only no-hitter ever recorded in the World Series. Joe DiMaggio called it the best-pitched game he ever saw as a player or spectator. Yogi Berra said he felt like a kid on Christmas morning. And Mickey Mantle said, "For one day, Don Larsen was the greatest pitcher in baseball history."

Now readers can relive that moment of greatness in the newest edition of *The Perfect Yankee*. With a deft pen and an announcer's enthusiasm, Larsen walks readers through each inning of that miraculous game. A must-read for any baseball fan.

$14.95 Paperback

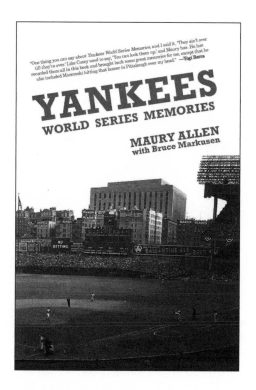

Yankees World Series Memories

by Maury Allen with Bruce Markusen

No two phrases in American baseball go together better than "World Series Champions" and "New York Yankees." The most iconic franchise in American sports, the Yankees have taken home 27 World Series titles. Out of the thousands of games and millions of memories that have come to define this epic team, Maury Allen has distilled the greatest championship moments in this newly revised edition of *Yankees World Series Memories*. The name says it all—within these pages readers can relive all the glory, passion, and excitement of Yankees domination. Critical reading for any baseball fan, *Yankees World Series Memories* is a nail-biting compendium of athleticism and skill. Readers young and old will relish tales of baseball's golden age and the thrill of modern victories. From Yogi Berra to Derek Jeter, Maury Allen highlights the absolute best of Yankees baseball.

$16.95 Hardcover